Like the Post-it® Note, *Conflict Communication* is something you never knew you needed but cannot live without. The materials are straight-forward and easy to apply, yet profoundly insightful. Once you begin to recognize the patterns that Miller describes within yourself and others it will forever change the way you interact. Armed with this new information I was able to resolve a longstanding deadlock on a $168M contract in less than two hours. It's amazingly powerful and wholeheartedly recommended.

—*Lawrence Kane, leader, ITI strategy, sourcing, and asset management at a Fortune 50® company*

CONFLICT COMMUNICATION

A New Paradigm
in Conscious
Communication

CONFLICT COMMUNICATION

A New Paradigm
in Conscious
Communication

Rory Miller

YMAA Publication Center
Wolfeboro, NH USA

YMAA Publication Center, Inc.
PO Box 480
Wolfeboro, NH 03894
800 669-8892 • www.ymaa.com • info@ymaa.com

ISBN: 9781594393310

Copyright © 2015 by Rory Miller
Cover design by Axie Breen
Edited by T. G. LaFredo
Illustrations provided by the author
POD 0117

Publisher's Cataloging in Publication

Miller, Rory.

Conflict communication : a new paradigm in conscious communication /
Rory Miller. -- Wolfeboro, NH USA : YMAA Publication Center, [2015]

pages ; cm.

ISBN: 978-1-59439-331-0 (print) ; 978-1-59439-332-7 (ebook)

At head of title on cover: ConCom.

Includes bibliographical references and index.

Summary: This book presents a functional taxonomy to see,
understand, and manipulate the roots of life's conflicts. You will have the
background, the principles, and a collection of tricks to manage and ideally
avoid dangerous conflicts. You may not realize that your reactions to conflict
are subconscious, scripted, and for the good of the group. Once recognized,
you can take actions that will reduce your being caught up in conflicts.--
Publisher.

1. Conflict management. 2. Conflict (Psychology) 3. Interpersonal
conflict. 4. Violence--Prevention. 5. Negotiation. 6. Problem solving.
7. Interpersonal communication. 8. Interpersonal relations. I. Title.
II. ConCom.

HM1126 .M55 2015   2015939009

303.6/9--dc23   1506

Printed in USA

CONTENTS

FOREWORD

BY MAJ GREGORY POSTAL, MD

The first principle [of scientific inquiry] is that you must not fool yourself—and you are the easiest person to fool.

—Richard P. Feynman,
Nobel Prize–winning physicist

Rory Miller has devoted many years to developing and refining strategies of conflict management. Those who know him can attest to the fact that while Rory has a heart of gold, when it comes to threat assessment and management he does not gladly suffer fools and seems incapable of allowing fatally flawed methods and theories to go unchallenged. In this we agree: as both a martial arts instructor and an Army psychiatrist I am acutely aware of the crucial roles that accurate prediction and effective strategies play when dealing with potentially violent individuals. Errors in either of these practices can have grave consequences, and Rory's work has certainly improved my practice and teaching of both.

In recent years, psychiatry has made considerable strides in some areas related to violence prediction, especially on an epidemiologic (macro) level. Law enforcement is clearly aided by improved accuracy in statistical predictions of the likelihood that an individual will recidivate after release from prison, or of how much danger is posed by someone who has made threats to a public figure. Despite this, psychiatry is abysmal as a field in terms of our ability to reliably predict or preempt incipient violence by patients. This deficiency becomes all too clear when one peruses data on assaults of clinicians or hears one too many times the assertion that if you work in the field "long enough" you will inevitably be victimized. Why is it that as a field of experts on human behavior we perpetually fail to become more competent in this crucial area?

One possible explanation is that the absence of good empirical data addressing violence on a "micro" level conflicts with our desire to utilize only scientifically proven methods in our work. While it is true that violence management is difficult to evaluate in a scientifically rigorous fashion (anyone want to volunteer to be in a placebo control group?), an insistence on relying only on data-driven methods can lead to lack of practice and trust in the skill sets we *do* have available to us. As a result, much like victims elsewhere, clinicians are often heard to say, "I should have trusted my gut" after they have been harmed. Also problematic is the lack of quality instruction on the nature of interpersonal violence, which sometimes results in a therapist continuing to try to "talk down" a patient beyond a point where there exists any reasonable chance of success. Exacerbating this trend have been various pseudoscientific programs of verbal de-escalation, which imply that resorting to physical intervention is by definition an indication of failure to comprehend or correctly implement that program's techniques.

A more likely reason for inadequately addressing the issue is the visceral aversion most people have to imagining a violent attack directed at them. The emotion of fear has played a crucial evolutionary role but has also created a compulsive tendency to avoid situations that make us feel scared or vulnerable. Ideally, when we recognize signs of danger, we respond in ways that increase our safety, avoiding the threat or proactively taking steps to minimize the potential for harm. When perceived threats in our environment cannot be eliminated, other methods must be relied upon to manage this intolerable anxiety. Historically, magical rituals or talismans had been utilized to ward off such fears; for most of us today this process has largely been internalized, functioning on a psychological rather than societal level.

Despite the fact that one could reasonably expect behavioral scientists to be in the forefront of the effort to develop better capacities for observing, understanding, and preventing violence, we too often also cling to a talisman of sorts: the fiction that we are *already* competent at dealing with violence. We know intuitively that were we to undertake a critical evaluation of how well our training has prepared us to address threats of violence, we would reveal dramatic deficiencies, bringing back full force that same sense of powerlessness and vulnerability. Is it any wonder, then, that so many of us avoid grappling with this issue?

In addition to the psychic distress resulting from becoming seriously disillusioned with a discipline to which one has devoted years, another disincentive is what Rory might term a "monkey fear": openly questioning whether your training has appropriately prepared you to manage violence will likely result in indifference from peers (at best) and condemnation from an organizational hierarchy that perceives a threat to the status quo. From the perspective of your supervisors, raising these issues not only impugns their expertise, it threatens to undermine their own sense of security on this issue. They may *initially* endeavor to explain to you how your anxiety about the threat of violence results from a lack of understanding, experience, self-confidence, etc., but should you persist in this questioning, you may quickly find you are becoming a pariah.

So how does all of this relate to this book (and to Rory's work in general)? While certainly based in science, what he presents here isn't *provable* in a strictly empirical sense. Furthermore, it would make a poor substitute "talisman of invulnerability," since that kind of absolute certainty in the face of a real threat is to a large degree what the ideas Rory presents here are designed to combat.

If, however, you are able and willing to tolerate the ambiguity (and vulnerability) inherent in any true threat assessment process *and* you can briefly set aside what you are sure you "know" about conflict, you can use this information to dramatically improve the likelihood you will avoid becoming a victim. When someone develops a scientifically proven and verifiable system, I will be first in line to sign up. For now, the closest we can come is what Rory presents here: a set of extremely effective tools for predicting, avoiding, and managing conflicts.

MAJ Gregory Postal, MD
Psychiatrist, Walter Reed Medical Center

FOREWORD

By Jack Hoban

Students of Japanese martial arts may be familiar with a formulation called *san-mitsu* (three mysteries), which is thought to be the path to enlightenment. In English, san-mitsu can be translated as "thought, word, and deed." And although it is believed that the three mysteries originated from Tibetan Buddhism, the concept is common to many spiritual philosophies, from Catholicism ("I confess to almighty God, and to you, my brothers and sisters, that I have greatly sinned, in my thoughts and in my words, in what I have done and in what I have failed to do . . .") to New Age-ism.

But my interest is martial arts, and we see the san-mitsu as the key to enlightened preservation of life. If you are reading this book, you may also be interested in protecting life—or at least in the art of resolving dangerous, and perhaps physical, conflict. We all may have thoughts on how to resolve conflict, and there are uncountable techniques pertaining to stopping (or winning or avoiding) a physical confrontation. But it may be the most underutilized of the three mysteries—words—that are the best tools for effective conflict communications. And that is why Rory Miller's new book, *Conflict Communication*, is so important. For herein are words you can use to resolve conflict.

Mr. Miller is well experienced when it comes to conflict—physical, verbal, and psychological. Rory is a seventeen-year veteran of a metropolitan correctional system. He spent eleven years as a CERT (Corrections Emergency Response Team) member. He has seen and dealt directly with more than his share of physical conflict. But it is his skill in verbal conflict resolution, highlighted in this book, that makes his lessons valuable for all of us—whether we are in one of the protector professions or dealing with the day-to-day verbal conflicts we encounter on the street, in business, with friends and family, with anyone.

Take Rory's characterization of the three aspects of the human brain: the lizard, the monkey, and the human. The lizard is inflexible and hardwired for survival; the monkey is all about the emotions. It is only when we use our human brains that we become optimal problem solvers and conflict resolvers. We need to know why this is so, and Rory explains why. And, when we are under extreme duress or emotionally agitated, we need to know how to trump the lizard and the monkey and use our human brains. Rory teaches us how. Finally, and of surprising importance, we need to know what our human brains can have us say that is proven to be effective in conflict situations. Rory teaches us the words that work—and warns us about the ones that don't. This why, how, and what of conflict communications are worth their weight in gold. They have been field tested in some very difficult environments, but they will work in virtually any kind of conflict. In other words, this book is for everyone; this book is for you and me.

Rory's material is important because it works, but there is even more to it than that. It is not enough just to say the right thing. Rory's approach is ethical—respectful of yourself and the lives of others, all others. When we speak calmly and respectfully, from our human brains, we do the right thing. Sometimes conflict is just a difference of opinion, and the respectful thing may be to just agree to disagree. But, in the real world, everybody isn't always right; in conflict situations there is often a party who is, well, wrong. But, even though the expert conflict communicator may have to correct immoral or illegal behavior, he or she shows respect for the lives of all others—through thought, word, and deed. The ability to deal with someone who is acting immorally or illegally—without disrespecting or "othering" that person—is a priceless skill that is available to you through reading this book. It is the key to being an adept problem resolver—and an ethical protector, for that matter.

Jack Hoban
President of Resolution Group International, subject matter expert for the US Marine Corps Martial Arts Program, and author of The Ethical Warrior

INTRODUCTION

How often have you found yourself in an argument with your wife, husband, or significant other and thought, "Here we go again"?

Have you ever found the answer to a real problem and had it ignored while the person you are trying to help wastes time and energy picking at you, trying to create a personal problem from a good thing?

Have you ever felt singled out and almost victimized for doing too well at a job?

The things that feel very personal are often impersonal. In the pages that follow, I'll do my best to explain the mechanisms that underlie so much of human conflict. I will try to give you tools so that you can see what is happening and choose another way. Most important of all, this book will help you avoid getting caught in the traps yourself. The two people who developed this program, Marc MacYoung and I, are not academics. We are not scientists. Between us, we have one undergraduate degree. But we do have extensive experience with conflict. Both of us have written well-received books on the subjects of violence and conflict, and both support families largely by teaching the nuances of physical conflict.

Strangely, working with violent, dangerous people is not that different from working with run-of-the-mill angry, annoyed, or selfish people. The difference is that the time compression (a violent person can set you up and execute his plan in seconds; a jealous coworker can work on his gossip campaign for weeks) can make the pattern easier to see. And the stakes, of course, make an incredible incentive to get good at talking things down. If talking fails, someone is going to bleed.

We both had track records for being skilled at talking people down. The question was whether it could be taught. That question got us looking at our successes and mistakes to find the underlying principles. The result of that quest was the original Conflict

Communications course, and this book.

The thing about a really good idea, a principle, is that it applies almost everywhere. As we worked out what was important and what had worked in the past, our students noticed that it didn't just apply to criminals and cops. The feedback for the first few classes made it clear: "Sure, this should work on the street, but you guys just explained my boss!"

Let me repeat something: we aren't scientists. Furthermore, there is very little good science in the study of conflict. Science, real science, isn't based on models or correlations, statistics or theories. It is based on experimental evidence—and no university ethics committee will ever approve an experiment that gets to the heart of fear, danger, and conflict. Not even at the emotional level that most people experience in day-to-day life.

Because we aren't scientists or theorists we don't want to present this as a theory. It is simply a model. There are theories presented in the book, some generally accepted, but none are true. No theory or model has a one-to-one correlation with the world. Maslow's hierarchy of needs is a powerful model for understanding conflict but has gaping holes as a theory.

Same with the overall theme of this work. Everything in here was back-engineered. What worked? Why did it work? *No idea.* Then think it through. What did the things that work have in common? *Oh, that reminds me of a theory from college; let me look it up. It worked.* It worked before it was ever a system. And it would continue to work as a model even if the underlying theories proved false. The only difference would be not knowing *why* it worked—and there is no guarantee that we know the real "why" now.

Most of what follows will be intuitively obvious. In a very real way, it is like teaching fish about water. Fish live in water. It affects everything the fish do—but it is invisible, and so whether the currents help or hinder swimming is largely a matter of chance. If the fish can be taught to see the water, they can use the most powerful element in their lives.

SECTION 1   BACKGROUND

It is easy to know things. If *Conflict Communications* were just a collection of tricks to memorize and use, we would need only section 3.

My experience is that *knowing* something is almost useless under stress, but *understanding* is often helpful. So section 1 is designed to give you the background, the concepts that underlie the program. If you understand the concepts and the principles (section 2), you can improvise under pressure—and the ability to improvise is probably the most valuable tool in dealing with conflict.

Section 1.1   Sex and Violence

There is a parallel between violence and conflict today and sex in the 1950s. In the 1950s polite people didn't talk about sex. Teachers did not discuss it in schools. No matter their private feelings on the subject, sex was denigrated as "dirty" and something that children should be kept ignorant of.

Today, despite the ritualized violence endemic to entertainment, children are not taught about conflict and certainly not taught about violence. They are told it is bad. How bad? So bad that under many grade-school zero-tolerance policies, even the victim of an assault is suspended. How does this differ from the treatment of a rape victim under Sharia law?

The extent of most of our education on the subject of conflict can be summed up in the single word: abstinence.

Does that work any better for violence than it does to limit teen sex? Understand that both sex and violence *will* happen. In what universe is ignorance of a problem an effective strategy?

This modern taboo has profound implications for managing conflict. The most profound is that it is difficult to solve a problem you are almost entirely ignorant about. You cannot work for peace while ignoring violence any more than a doctor can create treatments while refusing to study disease.

Another effect is that mediators and conflict professionals often bring profoundly unrealistic expectations to a problem. To think that there is always a reasonable solution is itself unreasonable. To imagine that there is always a win-win solution is to ignore the fact that for some people humiliating the victim (or watching the victim bleed) is part of the win.

By placing conflict into the realm of subjects that people don't talk about, ignorance and misinformation spread. The people who do experience violence and are willing to talk about it are marginalized, actively shunned. The tragedy of this taboo, like any other, is that it prevents the spread of information.

Freud postulated a three-level mind.

The id, he said, includes your fears and desires, your uncontrolled aggressions, your lusts and animal self.

The superego is, for want of a better word, your conscience. It is an amalgamation of everything you have been taught about how you *should* behave: what things are right, and what things are wrong.

The ego maintains a balancing act between the two. It is sweet reason. The "ego" is who you are.

That's what Freud thought.

Modern research blows much of this out of the water. The reasoning voice in your head, the thoughts you are aware of, is not *you*. You see things and make decisions, even complex decisions, very quickly. The reasoning mind plays catch-up. Your conscious thoughts are like the words on a computer screen. They are only indicators of what the machine is doing.

Freud got something right in all this, however. Sex and aggression may not be the most powerful drives in the human mind, but they are the two areas where what we have been taught and what we feel come into powerful conflict. How you resolve the emotions you feel with what you have been taught about right and wrong (or justice and vengeance) greatly shapes your personality. How you control or fail to control your desires is a big piece of who you are.

Very little of this is conscious.

What follows will include a lot of information about violence and conflict. Some of it will seem pretty academic. That's OK. The information is coming to you through the written word and will have to filter through your brain first.

That's only *OK*. It's not *good*. Just like sex, conflict is a thing of emotion. It is something that your gut already believes it understands. Conflict, and especially the higher level of violence, is very much a thing of emotions and feelings, of contact and connections. It is tactile and auditory, and olfactory—something you feel, hear, and smell as much as see.

So maybe, like sex, reading about conflict isn't the optimal way to get skilled at it. The optimal way, unfortunately, is to get involved in a lot of conflict and be lucky enough to survive, physically and emotionally, and then figure out what worked.

When we do sound academic, the science isn't that important. The concepts are important and you need to understand them. You need to understand them the way that you understand any other tool. This book isn't meant to be an exploration of theory. It is meant to be used.

Is violence bad? Is conflict bad? Are these questions even reasonable to you, or do they immediately provoke a response? *Of course* conflict is bad. *Of course* violence is bad. If those words sprang immediately to your mind, the very speed implies that they are emotional, not thoughtful reactions. They are things you have been conditioned to believe, just as sex was "dirty" sixty years ago—*of course*.

Section 1.2 Why and Wherefore—Maslow

In 1943, Abraham Maslow published his famous hierarchy of needs.

Maslow's Hierarchy of Needs

The idea is simple. If you are in danger of dying—starving, thirsty, sick, or about to be killed and eaten—that is your highest priority. Until you have taken care of your immediate survival needs, you don't care about and you don't waste resources on anything else.

Once your immediate physical needs are taken care of, you can start thinking about your physical security. How do you arrange to have food and water tomorrow and next week? How do you get shelter to protect you from the elements and from predators?

The next stage is the awkwardly titled "belongingness" need. Humans in the wild are poorly adapted to live alone. Providing all of the physical security needs is easier with a group, with tasks divided among several people. This is compounded by the fact that human children cannot survive alone. We are born into a family group of some sort and spend the rest of our lives in groups. Not only are few humans fit to survive alone, most can't even truly imagine being alone for any length of time. I can guarantee you that the most profound introvert you know reads or listens to music every day. Just because someone has trouble with the stress of interaction does not mean that he or she doesn't need the connection.

Almost as important as being in a group is knowing your place within that group. Maslow linked this to status in the group, being loved and respected. That's nice, but the need is deeper and less logical than that. Even being low status, a pariah, is less stressful than being unsure of your status. Most people have felt this uncertainty joining a new job or a new team or a new school. You're on board, maybe even have a title and official status, but you need to see where you fit with the social groups, the unofficial status hierarchy. Again, fitting in *somewhere* is far more important than *where* you fit in.

Lastly, according to Maslow, if all of these needs are fulfilled, an individual can self-actualize. You can live your dreams. Follow your heart. Write poetry or sculpt or do philanthropic work. Or you can live out your serial killer fantasies.

That's important. Not everyone shares your dreams. Not all humans draw joy from the same things. The patterns (whether of Maslow's hierarchy or the scripts we address later) are nearly universal. Their expression, however, can run the entire spectrum of human thought and feeling. If you give a man everything he needs, he will start looking for what he wants. What he (or she, men have no monopoly on this) wants may be to dominate or to destroy. You cannot simultaneously ignore this fact and deal with it.

You cannot simultaneously ignore problems and solve them.

Maslow's hierarchy creates a pyramid. The more vital something is to survival, the closer it is to the base.

Is conflict bad? Is violence bad? For much of our history as a species, both were necessary. Humans killed to eat, and fought to keep from being killed and eaten. Raiding for women, slaves, food, and plunder was common. Why? Because it worked. And it was easier than the toil of agriculture and raising children. It was always far easier to plunder Rome than to build Rome.

If you did not want to be a victim of violence, you used violence. This was a mathematical necessity. A tribe that didn't defend itself would be the easiest prey, therefore, the first choice; therefore, they would cease to exist, be slaughtered, or taken as slaves.

Skill at conflict and violence were survival traits until quite recently in human history. In some places they still are. In any place, they still can be under the right circumstances, such as a home-invasion crime in a normally peaceful neighborhood. It is hard for me to categorize something as "bad" that has kept my ancestors alive for millennia.

For most people in the industrialized world, the bottom two levels of the pyramid have never been a concern. It has been almost a century since the last time Americans had to worry about winter starvations or an epidemic killing thousands of people. It has been fifty years since Western Europeans had to worry about invading armies.

And so, most people in our modern industrialized society have absolutely no experience in dealing with conflicts stemming from the bottom two levels of this pyramid. Even hunger (a clear survival need) is now seen as a problem of social responsibility. The motivations and mechanisms of lower-level conflict are different from the mechanisms for the higher-social-level conflicts. And the social skills of conflict management do not transfer. Well, maybe about as well as your boxing skills will help with a cougar attack.

When big problems, like starving or being eaten alive by bears, fade, energy goes into other concerns. For most people, the conflicts they have been exposed to originate exclusively from the social levels of the pyramid: people trying to work their way into a group (and others trying to prevent this), or people bucking for position within the group.

This type of conflict, social conflict, rarely leads to serious violence. After all, it would be counterproductive to destroy a group you wanted to be part of, or to create so much hate and fear that you couldn't enjoy status. When social conflict does lead to extreme violence, such as a workplace or school shooting, the shooter is aware that he will not be getting a membership invitation from the group afterward.

However, because social conflict (belongingness and esteem on the pyramid) is the one area where people have some experience with conflict, it is easy to base beliefs about all types of conflict on this one type of experience.

Violence and conflict can be triggered from *any* level. An addiction can become so severe that it seems a matter of survival to get enough money for drugs, no matter who has to die. Robbing a victim of a car or jewelry or cash gets the criminal enough ahead to feel a few days' worth of security.

Extreme violence may be a gang initiation, and many subcultures bestow status on the "crazy" and the "hard." Violence for reputation isn't all that rare today and was common when dueling was part of being a "gentleman."

Lastly, there's the highest level of the pyramid: self-actualization. It was always implied in my college classes that the self-actualized person would be a good person, an artist and philanthropist and philosopher. Not true. Someone who is absolutely secure in his needs, both social and physical, will do whatever he desires and become what he wants to be. And if what he desires is to cause pain . . .

Violence can come from people as a whim or for fun or to live a fantasy. It can be profoundly self-actualizing. This hits one of my emotional buttons, because I was taught to believe self-actualization is a high, noble goal we all strive for. That twinge of emotion, that knee-jerk reflex that says bad people can't be self-actualized or that the higher forms of growth should be inherently noble is a sign that it is not my human brain, but my limbic system responding.

Conflict vs. Violence

Violence is a broad category with a lot of definitions. People can have violent emotions or speak violently. Physical violence is only one small aspect of violence, and violence is just an expression of conflict. Conflict is the big basket that holds all of these concepts.

Overt physical violence—the individual capacity for violence and assessing threat—is the subject of appendix 2.

Most readers may believe the fear they feel in any conflict is a deep fear that could turn physically violent. That isn't true. The fear comes from elsewhere.

Section 1.3 Why and Wherefore—Three Brains

There will be some scientific-sounding details in what follows. Feel free to ignore it. Unless you are doing research, the background science is not important. The concepts are.

Also remember (and this applies to many other areas of life, so pay attention) that this is a model. No model is perfect. No model directly reflects reality. In the words of George E. P. Box, "Essentially, all models are wrong, but some are useful."

As scientific theories, both Maslow's hierarchy and the triune brain theory have holes you could drive a truck through. If Maslow were correct, no hungry people could produce art and no soldier going into battle could write a poem.

The neuroscience of the brain is far more complex than three simplistic levels.

I really don't care. Properly applied, both models have amazing predictive power and give you a framework that allows you to see and manipulate the world around you. Can't speak for everybody, but I'll take "reliably useful" over "peer reviewed" every time.

For our purposes, you have three brains, which we will call the lizard, the monkey, and the human.

The *lizard* is the oldest part of your thinking brain, the hindbrain. Your survival instincts (particularly fight/flight/freeze responses) are triggered here. This is the part of your thinking brain most closely tied to your coordination, to your physical body and your senses. This is you, the animal.

The lizard also has an affinity for ritual and rhythm. Habits are laid down in this part of the brain, as are the little rituals that become mannerisms. I always add a little dash of coffee grounds to the pot, no matter how carefully I measured it. A friend starts every conversation with, "How's it going?" Our cat meows when he can see the bottom of the bowl. Habit and ritual.

Rhythm is often used to get in touch with this old part of the mind, as in tribal drumming and ecstatic dance. I noticed it another way though. When a criminal was getting adrenalized, losing his ability to reason as he got angrier and angrier, closer to exploding into violence, he would often develop odd little tics that were often rhythmic—shrugging his shoulders or bouncing on his toes. Humming.

The *monkey* brain corresponds to the limbic system, the emotional brain. The monkey is completely concerned with social behavior, with status and what other people might think.

The monkey cannot distinguish between humiliation and death. For much of our evolution, being cast out of the tribe was to be sentenced to a slow and lonely death. The monkey knows this and fears being ostracized above all things. Soldiers could not be relied on in wartime if the fear of being laughed at as a coward didn't override the fear of death.

You will see the power of the monkey in dangerous situations. In natural disasters or major events such as the Twin Towers' destruction, people were milling around, talking to each other, seeing what the other monkeys were going to do. In Baghdad, when an explosion went off nearby, some people would hit the floor. Some (who had been there awhile and could judge distance and safety) pretty much ignored it. Most looked around to see what they were supposed to do.

Because most of the conflict we experience comes from this level, the monkey scripts drive a lot of current human conflict behavior.

The neocortex, what we call the *human* brain, is the new kid on the block. It is thoughtful, usually rational (but only as good as its information). It is also slow. Gathering evidence, weighing options and possibilities, takes time. It tends to find a good solution, but usually one of the older sections of the brain has a decision all set to go before the neocortex has fully explored the problem.

You have three different brains with three different priorities. They evolved to deal with different kinds of conflict. They work using different scripts. They also have a very clear seniority system.

The lizard's only concern is your individual survival. It is utterly ruthless. It is also conservative and extremely resistant to anything new. This is why it is so hard, especially for people who have lived dangerous lives (such as victims of chronic child abuse) to change. *The lizard only cares about survival.* No matter how hard life has been, how dangerous it is, or how clearly it seems that a bad ending is inevitable, all the lizard knows is that what you are doing hasn't gotten you killed yet. Any change might.

This can be especially obvious in moments of extreme fear. When a rookie officer tries the same wristlock again and again even though it is not working. An officer repeats over and over, "Drop the weapon, drop the weapon," when it is clear he has no choice but to shoot; the lizard is freezing him into a loop. The lizard assumes it is a survival loop because it hasn't gotten you killed—yet.

Most people only experience the lizard in moments of extreme terror, if at all. This means they associate it with the survival stress response, the cascade of stress hormones that floods your body under extreme threat. The stress hormones affect your vision and hearing, your memory, your coordination, and your judgment. The stress hormones may make you clumsy, with tunnel vision, functionally deaf, stupid, stubborn, and incapable of remembering anything.

People who have only experienced the lizard under these conditions assume the lizard is clumsy and stupid. Not so. An elite athlete "in the zone" is functioning almost wholly in the lizard brain. Watch a kid playing a video game he or she has mastered and you see the lizard brain, totally absorbed in a task.

Those who have had their lizard triggered without a massive dose of adrenaline have sometimes been shocked by their own cold, ruthless thought processes. Some postevent stress among survivors may come from a realization that what one is willing to do to survive is not compatible with self-image or even with internalized concepts of right and wrong. People start talking about a beast or a shadow or a "gray man" inside of them. Some obsess on it.

This part of your brain is not alien. Nor is it wrong. Not any more wrong than a rat, cornered, fighting like a cornered rat. If the rat had your brain, it would use it. For most of our evolution, this deep brain was on tap and used. It got some exercise and we (meaning the rest of our brains) were familiar with it.

As the oldest and concerned with the very highest priority,

survival, the lizard brain has the chemical power to completely take over your brain. It can hijack you whenever it feels the need. This hijacking is triggered by fear of imminent death.

The Lizard, the Monkey, and Death

The lizard is only concerned with survival and outranks the monkey, so how can there be soldiers? Why doesn't the lizard keep people from getting into the position of choosing between status and survival?

It's because the lizard cannot deal with abstract concepts. The idea that a mortar might hit you has no meaning, no immediacy to the lizard. Once the lizard has heard the whistle and seen an explosion, the example becomes real.

Then, though it might run, it has also learned that the training worked. Once the lizard trusts the training, you can get a hyperefficient soldier.

The monkey is concerned with social survival and status. It literally cannot distinguish between humiliation and death.

This is a key point in many very serious issues. At a low level, you can see it in action by taking a group of friends out bungee jumping. Fear of falling is one of the two fears that appear to be hardwired into human infants (the other is loud noises). In bungee jumping, there is a small but real risk of injury. It usually takes a few minutes of cajoling to get a timid person to jump. A risk taker or adrenaline junkie will not need much encouragement but will usually hesitate just before making the leap. It takes an act of will, of some degree, to overcome one of the deepest genetic fears humans have.

Afterward, take the same group of friends out to a karaoke bar and try to get them to sing. Some absolutely won't. A few will, if they have performed before. For most it will take alcohol, insults, teasing, all to overcome a fear of . . . what?

What a bunch of drunk strangers will think? Not even that, because two beers later the drunk strangers won't even remember your singing.

11

Why is this fear, this imaginary fear of what other people *might* think, so powerful?

Make no mistake, it is powerful. In his book *Machete Season*, Jean Hatzfeld documents a man in the Rwandan genocide who went out every morning to hunt Tutsi and hack them up—men, women, and children—with machetes. The man said the taunts and jeering and laughter if he *didn't* join in were much worse, "like a poison." It was easier to chop humans up than to be laughed at for not chopping humans up.

The monkey is powerful, and it explains some very deep, very dangerous puzzles in human behavior, conflict, and trauma.

The physical injuries from rape often heal quickly. The psychic scars take much longer, if they heal at all—because the monkey brain's view of how the world should work, the things that can and can't happen, how people treat each other, is shattered.

That people stay in a clearly abusive relationship is a puzzle, but not for the monkey. The monkey knows it is still a relationship. To have a tribe and a place, no matter how painful, is less terrifying than to be alone or to be uncertain of your place.

Listen to those words: painful, terrifying. The monkey is the seat of emotions. There are deeper emotions. The lizard understands a pure joy in the physical world that rarely makes it to the conscious mind. The lizard also understands a primal fear of extinction. These emotions are intense and, in my experience, two of the few emotions that don't require people. It is hard to get jealous of a bicycle, or to hate a rock. The third nonmonkey emotion appears to be wired to the human brain, the neocortex, and that is *curiosity*.

The monkey, however, lives on the social nuances of emotion.

It is less afraid of dying than of being seen as a coward, of shame. The monkey turns honest grief into self-pity. Sometimes it turns lizard fear into rage, and that can be a profound survival strategy, but the monkey can also produce rage in response to an imagined insult.

It is not always negative. The connections with family, friends, and our sense of belonging to any group trigger at the monkey level. It allows compassion, patriotism, self-sacrifice, and a desire to make a better future for others. The monkey is the one who can feel the concept of a community.

Sometimes, guided and influenced by the human brain, it is rational and altruistic. Even when it is not, the monkey mind feels rational. This is a huge danger.

Dr. Drew Westen, in his book *The Political Brain*, writes about a study in which people who label themselves "conservative" or "liberal" are asked to explain their political views. They feel logical. They sound logical. But their neocortex (where logic resides) isn't even active. The activity is in their limbic system, their emotional centers. Their monkey brains.

When you label yourself, by nationality or creed or political party or business affiliation or social club, you are in your monkey brain. No matter how rational you feel, the label has the specific purpose of identifying you within a tribe and preventing you from thinking rationally.

Because, if you notice a pattern here, all of these obviously silly or inefficient monkey strategies (staying in bad relationships, hacking up others, fear of humiliation, labeling) *do* work. They don't just work for *you*. They work to keep the groups together.

We like to think our human mind is who we really are. We like to think we spend a lot of time there. Get over that.

The lizard and the monkey both work at a level below words. You can think of it as subconscious. Words are symbols, imprecise and slow. The human mind is the master of words and symbols. Words have great power in explaining our actions to others—and to ourselves.

Research has shown, very consistently, that in many cases decisions are made subconsciously, before the conscious, human brain has even finished evaluating the question.

If someone asks, "Which of these shirts do you like best?" your subconscious mind will have chosen one before your conscious mind really starts to compare them. When you are asked why you chose one, your conscious mind will have an answer—an answer completely invented well after the decision was made.

Much of the time spent in our human mind is spent making up reasons for what we (the other two minds) already believe or have already decided. Sometimes we are explaining it to others. Often we are explaining it to ourselves. As long as there is no friction, as long as our explanations work well enough that our map of reality isn't obviously whacked, our brains don't care whether our explanations are accurate.

That's right. We only care that we are lying to ourselves if it gets us in trouble later. Frankly, the monkey and the lizard don't give a damn about explanations.

Despite its slowness, its capacity for self-delusion, and the ease with which it can be hijacked, the human brain is extremely powerful. The human brain solves problems. That's what it does.

The lizard brain doesn't understand abstract reasoning, but the human brain uses abstract reasoning as a tool. The human brain juggles symbols—words and numbers—to learn and to create art and invent. Often, the monkey brain can't distinguish the symbols from what they represent, and that is the basis of sympathetic magic.

How do we get these supplies over the border? Why isn't the car starting? What do these symptoms mean?

How do I reach my goal?

I believe that only the human mind can understand an abstract goal and work toward it. The monkey and the lizard, despite their strengths, are purely reactive. And it is my gut feeling (I can't point to a study) that the lizard lives in the now, with no thought of the future. And the monkey can only envision bad outcomes. Both seem incapable of imagining a better future.

Section 1.4   Types of Conflict

Humans, like other animals, have completely separate mechanisms for using force within our own species and on other species.

Two male rattlesnakes vie for territory by wrapping around each other in a single coil and wrestling to see who is stronger. They kill prey, however, by lying in wait and biting the prey, injecting the hapless mouse or bunny with poison.

Bears, tigers, wolves, and elk all have ritualized dominance games. They look like fights, but they almost never result in serious injury. Elks clash antler to antler, not antler to ribs.

Animals do not use the same tactics against other species they use within their species. The predators go for the quickest, safest kill that they can. The elk as a prey species prefers to run, but when cornered, its primary weapons are hooves, not seasonal antlers.

Humans are the same. We have ritualized patterns for social conflict and social violence. When dealing with creatures outside the species, we simply butcher them or hunt them. It is far easier to kill something that looks different from you than something that looks like you. Even a vegetarian will reflexively swat a mosquito.

This is nature, and this is the dividing line between social and asocial conflict.

Social conflict is what happens within a group. Millennia ago, the group would be a tribe or village. Almost everyone was related and you would know the same people from birth to death. Today, the group might be a company or a club or a team or task force or a family. The mechanisms for dealing with problems haven't changed. Neither have the problems that are dealt with.

Social conflict stems from a handful of needs:

1. To create and maintain a social group.

Humans generally don't do well alone in the wild. It is a big world, full of things with sharper teeth and claws, weather that can freeze or bake us, wildfires, and disease. Babies cannot survive without nurturing and training. All humans have been conditioned from birth to find their identity in a group.

Having a group, being in a group, and keeping the group going are immensely powerful drives in our evolution. A human alone could expect death by starvation or hypothermia, death from predators, and enslavement or death from other humans.

A tribe that fell apart—that either disintegrated and separated, or became incapable of acting together—became an easy mark for a more integrated tribe or band of raiders. Again, the result was slavery or death and assimilation for the survivors into the new, stronger tribe.

2. To establish and maintain a hierarchy within the group.

Knowing your place in your group is just as important as having a group to begin with. Much has been made of status and "climbing the social ladder," but very little social conflict comes from direct rivalry for the leadership position. In some species where only a small percentage of the males mate, constantly attempting to increase status and power makes sense. That is less true with humans.

With humans, the stress often comes from uncertainty of place. You see this in kids when they go to a new school or when people move to new areas or change jobs, or even transfer to a new division within the same organization.

Our official rank in the hierarchy has very little to do with our place in the hierarchy. A senior officer transferred from patrol to street crime knows who he is on paper—his rank, seniority, training, and experience—but even in a highly regimented, readily apparent rank structure, the real questions aren't satisfied. Will the cliques be the same in the new assignment? Which clique, if any, will he fall into? The hard chargers? The regular guys? The desk jockeys? The sycophants? The outsiders?

And what will his role be in the clique? The leader? The *consigliere* (advisor)? The chaplain (shoulder to cry on)? The joker? The tech geek? The muscle? The reliable? The pleaser?

These are the things our monkey brains need to know in order to be comfortable, to be safe. There is a lot to think about here. Is the clique important or the role? Are you more comfortable being the leader of the tech geeks or the pleaser/gopher in the hard chargers?

I have seen people who so needed to join a particular group that they did not care what their role was, and watched them scramble, trying to be the clown, the pleaser, and even the eye candy ("Maybe I can't fight, but my uniform is always pressed."). And I have seen people who, no matter what group they were in, always fell into the role of advisor, chaplain, or leader.

Many social conflicts do not come from two rivals attempting to get ahead by pulling the other down. That does happen, especially where resources, such as promotions, are limited. More comes from people establishing their territorial right to be in a role. As an example, one of the most common causes of friction, especially among young men who are drinking, is someone being funny. It happens because there is someone in that group who already has an identity as the joker. If a stranger is funnier than he is, especially if the stranger is outgoing and seems capable of fitting in with the group, the established joker will need to assert his place. It will start with funny insults and rapidly get personal. It may follow the monkey dance (see section 2.2) to the edge of blows. The joker's friends will pull them apart, and that is the key. By pulling the joker back, the group has chosen him by physical contact. The hierarchy is established. Change is prevented.

Any change in personnel—new people added, people assigned to work with new groups, or people leaving—puts these established hierarchies at risk. The monkey brain finds that quite stressful.

3.   To enforce the mores of the group.

Mores (pronounced like the moray eel) are the attitudes and beliefs of a given group. The way things are done, how things are seen. The rules.

The mores define the group. Without them, there is no difference between *them* and *us*. Without that difference, there is no group. The human primate needs a group.

Put that starkly, the primate need for a group can seem silly and unnecessary. Why can't we just jettison our mores? Give it a try if you want. Just remember that believing there is something wrong with murder and rape are mores. The idea of doing a good job is a more. Paying your bills, and the electric company's obligation to supply electricity to your house, are mores.

I've been in parts of the world where some of these mores are not shared. I like it better where they are.

Because there is no group without group identity, mores tend to be rigorously defended, which means conflict. How rigorously? That depends on socialization of the members within the group, and how strongly they agree with the rules.

17

In a well-run group (company or family or team) where the personnel know the rules and believe in them, a quizzical look or at most a short conversation is all that is required. In other groups, depending on the rule broken and the message the leadership wants sent, the transgression could be "corrected" with a savage beating or a brutal death. Death is always to send a message to the others, obviously. The dead man or woman learns nothing.

This is not something esoteric. You do this within your own family. This is how children are socialized. They learn the rules of both the family and society at large by being punished when they violate the mores. It might be handled with a stern look, a loss of privileges, or a spanking, depending on the mores of the group (how punishment is meted out is also a more) and the socialization level of the child.

Asocial conflict is applied outside the species or group.

Outside the species includes hunting, butchering livestock, eradicating dangerous animals, and even swatting flies.

Different people have different attitudes about the universal value of life, but that value, with few exceptions, is scaled to how similar or dissimilar a life-form is. People who raise their own food rarely name the animals they intend to eat. (Actually, I do tend to name livestock, but on the order of naming a calf Hamburger.)

One thing is nearly universal: hunting or butchering or swatting flies is done with the goal of maximum efficiency. The animal is dead as quickly and safely as possible. It is not a contest (except in the mind of sportsmen) or a show. It is a utilitarian quest for protein. There is no attempt to prove to the lamb that you are his social superior. It *is* emotional to kill a large animal (the first fifty times or so) but it is not egotistical, not about who is boss. It is a chore.

We will discuss it later, but it is very, very rare for a human to bring this level of dispassion to another human. When one can, he can kill quickly and without remorse or hesitation.

> Social and asocial are hard divisions. There is not a scale.
>
> There is, however, a blending.
>
> The difference: You will never find anything that is 30 percent social and 70 percent asocial. But you will find asocial violence that is milked for social payoffs and vice versa. The criminal example is a serial rapist or cold-blooded killer who brags about it to score points with his friends.
>
> And you will frequently find people who hunt every year with their friends, but the primary purpose is the bonding. Getting protein is a secondary goal.

War is an interesting case. It is extremely social violence in that it is fought by groups and for the good of the group. At the same time, historically, it is nearly always fought for resources—for land or plunder. Those are asocial motivations.

War requires killing, and the asocial efficiency of butchering or hunting would seem to be appropriate, but wars are fought by people against people, and many of the soldiers will feel the humanity of the enemy.

In an attempt to engage in asocial violence socially, training soldiers requires intense bonding. Performance in combat relies on the limbic system's overpowering logical thought and, to a certain extent, survival instinct. The soldier must be more afraid of letting his buddies down or being labeled a coward than of dying. Those are social motivations.

This mix, an attempt to use asocial-level violence on another human and using social pressures to make it possible, make war and raiding ripe for cognitive dissonance on many levels.

Othering is the ability to convince yourself that another human is different from you. In most cases the ability to other determines how much force can be used on another person.

Propaganda in war or mass rallies in a police state are attempts to co-opt the monkey mind—the limbic system—into believing that the enemy is not a person, not like us, not one of us.

If you can be convinced that the enemy is not human, you can butcher or hunt a person just as if he were an animal. If you are truly convinced, not just following the crowd with your monkey mind, you will not even suffer from guilt reactions.

That depth of belief is rare. It is hard to look at a person as he dies and truly believe he is not a person.

Some people do it naturally. Antisocial personality disorder is a description of a certain personality type that really doesn't care about other people. Almost all violent criminals test out as having ASPD. A person with extreme antisocial personality disorder doesn't seem to acknowledge other humans as real. A few can kill with all the emotional trauma you experience playing a video game.

For some people, othering is a skill. A new criminal usually has to work himself up to an act of violence, talk himself into it. He convinces himself he is only taking what should be his by right, if the world were fair, or tells himself a story where his victims are the bad guys.

Police officers and soldiers, especially the extremely professional veteran, other by behavior. "This person did X, which elicits Y force." "If I see A, I will do B under the rules of engagement." The ability to other by behavior is one of the most important skills in force professions. It prevents overreactions (whether excessive-force complaints or atrocities). Because it is not personal, it removes the monkey mind from the equation. It also prevents, in my experience, burnout. Having an emotional connection, whether that connection is love or hate, increases the stress of a force incident. Othering by behavior allows one to maintain absolute respect for an enemy or a threat, even if it is necessary to kill.

Not being othered is also a skill, and one that is critical in de-escalating potentially violent situations. (See section 3: Tactics, Tools, and Techniques.) All of the information in section 1 is background to establish this: *Your responses to conflict are subconscious, scripted, and for the good of the group.*

SECTION 2   FUNDAMENTALS

Your natural responses to conflict are subconscious, scripted, and for the good of the group.

They do not serve you. They do not serve the task or the job.

They do follow predictable patterns. For the most part, these patterns are invisible. You do not see the game you are playing any more than a fish sees the water it swims in. Seeing the invisible, and teaching others to see it, may seem difficult. It isn't. There is nothing new in this book. Even if you have never consciously seen this process, you have lived it. Just as the hum of your refrigerator doesn't keep you awake at night, you are not aware of something so constant.

One example: Every long-term couple I know has at least one, and usually several, arguments they have word for word, periodically. We know these arguments are subconscious. No one turns to his wife and says, "Honey, let's have that argument we have every other week. You know, argument 2B, the one about rinsing the dishes." No one chooses these: *Subconscious.*

We know they are scripted for a couple of reasons. Primarily, every so often you become conscious enough to recognize the argument. You know exactly what you are going to say and exactly how your significant other is going to respond. But have you ever tried to just walk away? It is almost as if something pulls you back in, compels you to finish the script: *Scripted.*

What took us forever to figure out: *Who is this making happy?* A simple flatworm, which doesn't have a brain to speak of, will move away from pain. If this argument annoys us, why does it perpetuate? It's not making you happy. It's not making your spouse happy. *So, why?*

To your human brain, this repeating argument is an unresolved issue. But to your monkey brain, it is the signifier of stability. Stability is desired by your limbic system far more than happiness. If you have been having the same argument every week for five years, your monkey knows the relationship is stable. Even the bad things don't change. You may be unhappy, but the tribe is safe.

Your reactions to conflict are *subconscious, scripted,* and *for the good of the group*.

Section 2.1 Responses to Conflict Are Subconscious

In a way, this statement isn't fair. Most of our thoughts, reactions, and even beliefs are not conscious. They are not decisions, or even things we know.

The words in our heads are our conscious thoughts. These are the thoughts we are aware of. There is much more going on in our brains. There always has been and always will be. I equate the words in my head to the words on a computer screen—just a very tiny picture of many deeper things that are going on.

Someone insults you and you get angry. What just happened? Insults are things that make us angry or ashamed or defensive. That pretty much defines an insult. Which came first? Did the words used hurt my feelings? Or did the words become an insult because of my feelings? Which came first, the chicken or the egg?

That's not the important part. The important part is that nowhere in the process did your conscious mind come into play. Nothing was a decision. He said the words. You did not then think, "He said this, which implies that, which might cause me some problem if I did not respond with enough emotion." He said the words; you felt the emotion. Likely, you acted on the emotion or at least showed your feelings well before you thought.

In emotion this is somewhat easy to see. We also subconsciously react to other things, sometimes elaborately, without thinking about them. We will talk about scripts later, but they make a good example here:

The broken record: In any long-term relationship—work, parent/ child, or spouse—the pair falls into disputes that are nearly the same word for word each time:

"Clean your room."

"Mom, I can't. I have homework!"

"Why didn't you do your homework yesterday? You had all

weekend."

"I was busy yesterday."

"You spent the whole day on the phone. Clean your room!"

"But Mom . . ."

"I'm tired of hearing the same old excuses."

Or:

"Wilkes, I need the Fischer file."

"I'm on it."

"You always say you're on it. When will it be done?"

"Just a few, Chief."

"A few what? Jesus! You're like talking to my five-year-old."

"I never get tired of hearing that, Chief."

Or the cop classic, after patting down someone and finding a 35mm canister of meth in his pocket:

"Mind telling me what this is?"

"I don't know, Officer."

"It was in your pocket."

"These aren't my pants, Officer."

These are all complex interactions. They are conversations, and they happen in words. You know how they start and you know how they end. You know them word for word, by heart.

So tell me: if you are having the same argument in the exact same words with your wife or teenager or employee every week, how's that working? It's not working and you would know it's not working if you gave it a half second of thought.

But you do it anyway. The only explanation is that you didn't even give it a half second of thought. Going into the script was automatic.

Your responses to conflict are subconscious.

Section 2.2 Your Responses to Conflict Are Scripted

Those were some examples of scripting in day-to-day, low-level friction, but the scripts go deeper.

In my book *Meditations on Violence*, I described the monkey dance. Animal species have ritualistic dominance behavior to establish territory or status between males. It is ritualistic, stylized, and designed to limit injury to the participants.

The human equivalent is the monkey dance. It is not just the fistfight you might imagine, but all of the steps leading up to the fight.

It begins with a hard stare, which is followed by a verbal challenge (often, "What are you lookin' at?"). The verbal back and forth can go on for some time, or the ritual can be ended with an apology and submissive body language.

If the dance is not ended, one or both of the participants will close the distance. It is completely subconscious, but most will "puff up," trying to look bigger, spreading their chest muscles and coming up on their toes. Sometimes they bob up and down like roosters. The verbal interplay continues.

Once they have closed distance, an apology still works. If one backs down, then dominance is established and the monkey dance is over. What both parties are actually hoping for is that friends will intervene and pull them apart. If that happens, dominance isn't established per se, but both have established their willingness to defend status and territory. They can then coexist in the same space with mutual respect.

If they are not separated and neither backs down, the next stage is contact. It will usually be a two-handed push to the chest or an index finger poke to the chest. In some cultures you knock the hat off. In almost any culture, if the contact is poking his nose with your index finger, the fight is on.

The next step is the fight, but it isn't a very skilled fight. It is usually a series of looping punches aimed at the top and side of the head—exactly the kind of thing more likely to damage the hand of the person punching than the person being punched.

There are also many strategies for circumventing the script, but that concept comes later.

One of the keys to understanding that this is a script is that even trained fighters fall into this pattern, knowing full well (with their human brains) that it is a stupid way to fight.

Robert Twigger, in his book *Angry White Pyjamas*, describes the senior-most instructors of Yoshinkan Aikido on an epic pub crawl after the death of their founder. By the end of the night, these masters of aikido wound up in a brawl—throwing wild punches and rolling around on the floor. These weren't just dojo ballerinas. These were the men responsible for teaching the Tokyo riot police.

Another common, very dangerous script is the pattern of domestic violence. With tension building, an incident of abuse, and then a period of relative peace, only the people inside the cycle are ever surprised.

These scripts are old and predate language. Even chimpanzees have patterns to deal with conflict and aggression. When a high-status chimp is abusive to a lower-status chimp, he or she will make a point to spend extra time grooming the lower-status member later.

Like the primates we are, if a boss is out of line with a subordinate, there will be a reconciliatory gesture later. It might be small and halfhearted, but it will be there. It will not happen because the boss thought about his actions, developed a sense of guilt, and tried to alleviate the guilt. Those thoughts may occur, but they have almost nothing to do with the action. That is the human brain making explanations for what the monkey has already decided must be done. The gesture will be made because there will be a niggling feeling of unfinished business until the script is completed.

Same with the monkey dance. Many men, in their later years, do not remember the fights they won or lost as children. They are often haunted by the ones they ran away from.

Scripts are pervasive and cover almost all areas of human interaction. Falling in love is a script with specific steps and requirements. It is a script that can be manipulated.

"Hi, I'm Bill," starts a script. If the other person doesn't offer a name in return, the unfinished-business feeling will be there. On both sides. Try it.

Your responses to conflict (and many other things) are scripted.

Section 2.3 For the Good of the Group

Usually scripts are beneficial, or at least harmless. The constant daily drone of small talk, the ritual greetings, even venting anger or complaining about politics or foreign affairs that we have no direct knowledge of, are all comforting. It's the soothing background noise of a group without a pending crisis.

Sometimes the script does not benefit you as an individual: the bloody nose at the end of a monkey dance. The codependent partner who stays in the abusive relationship. The junior member of a criminal gang who does time for a crime to protect a more senior member (a peculiar sense of loyalty in that the situation never reverses).

Even the argument you have had a hundred times with your partner, the one that never gets solved. You get frustrated, feeling like you are stuck in a broken record.

It doesn't benefit you. In many cases it doesn't benefit anyone. Is anyone happy and satisfied in an abusive relationship? In a dysfunctional office or family? Even when we know it is dysfunctional, we keep doing the same things over and over again. We are on a script.

If the script doesn't benefit anybody, why do we do it?

We do it because the monkey brain believes it benefits everybody. It benefits the group.

The monkey brain feels it is a survival necessity to be in a group. It is nearly as important to know one's place in the group. Once these are established, no matter how horrible it may be (the daughter who is the target of abuse is not in what one would call a high-status role in a nice group), the monkey is afraid that changing anything may change everything. And the monkey sees that as death.

The Lizard, the Monkey, and Change

As anyone who has left an abusive relationship or tried and failed to leave one can tell you, change is hard—even change where every ounce of your being knows that change is needed or very bad things will happen.

The monkey is afraid of social change. Being Quasimodo in Notre Dame is better than being Quasimodo with nowhere to go. Being the red shirt on *Star Trek* is better than not being on the show. Being the teased and humiliated mascot of a clique is better than being alone. This is how the monkey responds, and it takes courage and discipline to walk away from something real, even if it is bad, to something unknown.

The lizard is worse. You need to understand this if you wish to help people who have lived in violent or dangerous environments. The lizard only cares about personal survival. If it has been through very dangerous times, the lizard only knows two things:

You are alive.

What you have done in the past has not gotten you killed.

The lizard believes, especially when it senses danger, that any departure from past behavior is a step into an unpredictable minefield. *That* might be better, but *this* has never gotten you killed.

This is why it is so hard to leave abusive relationships. This is why people who survived abusive relationships as children so often seek them as adults. This is why, sometimes, when a killer is attacking a victim, the victim doesn't run or fight but just keeps saying the same thing over and over. This is one of the reasons it is so difficult to leave the gang lifestyle.

With the lizard and the monkey both fearing change, it can take an extreme act of human will to do the right thing.

The scripts benefit the group by ensuring stability. That repeated argument you have with your significant other? Your human brain is stressing about a problem left unsolved. Your monkey brain is comforted: if you have been having the same argument for five years, the relationship has gone five years without serious change. All is well.

27

What do the scripts do? They do the things the monkey brain concentrates on. They handle the interactions for most of Maslow's social levels.

They establish hierarchies. Your monkey brain likes hierarchies and roles. It likes to know who is in charge under what circumstances. Kids know which adult to go to with different types of problems. Kids are incredibly stressed when they move to a new school because they need to learn a new hierarchy.

They identify a group as a coherent tribe. If you can't define or identify the group, there is no group—and the monkey panics. The identity of a tribe is not in what its members do, but in how they do it and the symbols or stories they use. Every group through all of history had to carry water. There's no identity in that, but carrying it in a skin bag, a tightly woven basket, or a bucket is part of who you are. And whether that bucket or basket is decorated and how.

It is important for rules to differ. You see this especially in religions. Religion can be a sensitive subject, so I'll try to tread lightly: the moral bases of most religions are basic common sense. There are relatively few ways for groups of people to get along. Be nice to each other. Don't lie or steal or murder. There's not a lot of cultural identity in common sense, so the common sense has to be wrapped in something to make it special. Dietary restrictions. Scheduled prayers. Special clothes. Grooming requirements. These are the things that identify the group, and there will be special rules to maintain the identifiers.

You can follow every ethical precept in the Christian Bible, but unless you believe a God-man was born, crucified, and came back to life three days later, you aren't a Christian. Conversely, if you believe that, you are a Christian, even if you flaunt the ethical code.

On a deep level, we know that integrated, coherent groups survive better than fragmented or disjointed groups. Strong cultural identity is a powerful survival trait. People have been trying to exterminate the Jews for thousands of years, but they still have a strong identity and still exist. Where are the Babylonians? The Assyrians?

Understand that all of the individuals die, but the group continues. A group without these ties is easier to conquer, eradicate, or enslave. The markers of membership will never be common sense because there is not enough difference in common sense to distinguish your tribe from another.

What is the difference between the Crips and the Bloods? Whether they kill over red bandanas or blue bandanas, it's about *which* symbols they're willing to kill for. But if one group were not willing to kill over the symbols (because they were too logical) and the other group were willing, the first group would disappear. Eradicated or absorbed.

There are some things where causality is moot. It does not matter if circumstances drive this factor or if it is inborn—if the only way to survive is with X, all survivors will have X, whether they were born with it or learned it.

Because of this, people will often die and kill for symbols or ideals more readily than for material things. And questioning one of the identity markers is felt as a direct attack, not just on the person but on his or her tribe or family.

Scripts also establish and maintain the rules. Every group has social norms—ways that people do and don't interact, things you may and may not do. These rules are important because they define the group. Different types of groups deal with rule enforcement in different ways. These are heavily influenced by socioeconomic class, culture, and the functionality of the group.

In an extremely functional group, whether a tactical team or a happy family, the members believe in the basic purpose of the group and agree on the rules and the value of the rules. When a rule is broken, it is often an oversight or a special case, and all that is usually required is a reminder of the rules.

My son starts to argue with his mother and I raise my eyebrow. He loves his mom; he just needed a reminder he overstepped. He apologizes. Problem solved. This is a script.

In a less functional group, which can be defined as a group where the members don't buy into the norms, the dynamic is different. Fewer of the transgressions are oversights. Many are challenges either to the hierarchy or the rules themselves. Members of the hierarchy—senior members or enforcers—punish the transgressor. The punishment is intended to be an additional reason to behave. It is also used to send a message.

How harsh the punishment will be is a measure of how dysfunctional the group is or how fearful the hierarchy is of losing control.

> Level of willing membership plays a key role in what effectively corrects behavior. If the transgressor genuinely believes in the basics of the society, a reminder is enough.
>
> If someone is challenging those basics, it is a qualitative, not a quantitative difference. In a predator or someone who has taken on the identity of an outlaw, the low-level stuff, like reminders and counseling, are treated by the outlaw as proof of weakness. For him, low-level reprimands encourage more rule breaking.
>
> If someone chooses to other the rest of the world, correcting behavior is an entirely different challenge than helping someone see his or her mistake.

The scripts don't only punish wrongdoing. They are there to establish what is normal as well. That means they will also come into play when someone does too well.

If you've worked high-risk stuff, you have probably noticed that it seems like the best operators spend more time in the commander's office explaining successful actions than screw-ups do explaining mistakes.

We assumed, like most people do, that it was corrective. Punishment. One of the tenets of leadership is "Praise in public; criticize in private." Since we were being called to the office, it was private. Therefore it was punishment. Therefore, we did something seen as wrong. If the only thing we had done was a very good job, doing a good job must be wrong. We would go into the meeting defensive, thinking words like "professional jealousy," or that we were being punished for making others look bad.

It's not just a cop thing. It happens everywhere. Software and IT professionals report the same thing. Researchers and maintenance staff with incredible work ethics.

It has nothing to do with punishment. We'll talk about different kinds of groups later, but for now understand that the people who call you into the office have a primary goal of keeping the group together with absolute minimum change. This is not in their job description; it is deeper than that. At a certain level in any big organization, the function changes to preserving the organization, which means not just survival but limiting change.

Drawing attention of any kind, good or bad, brings you to the office. Not to punish you. Not even to get you to conform. It is purely an attitude check to make sure that (1) you are still a member of the group and (2) you know your place within the group.

That simple. You see, screw-ups can do a lot of damage to the group, and they need to be checked. Do they know the rules and norms? Does the screw-up buy into them? Then he is probably salvageable.

But extraordinary people sometimes leave the group. They break away. That causes change and to the monkey, all change comes with risk. If it is a young or new member, that's cool. The person is just trying to increase value and move up in the hierarchy. That follows the normal pattern, the normal script.

An established member who does an extraordinary job but has no urge to move up the ladder is an unusual pattern. This person will be called into the office again and again. Not to punish, not to harass, but because the pattern doesn't make sense, especially to someone who values rank and status.

It is an attitude check. If it were a group of dogs, it would involve a lot of butt sniffing.

The scripts also limit change by preventing breakaways and preventing serious violence.

The monkey dance, for instance, is not serious violence. In the rare instance where someone dies, it is almost always because one of the participants falls and hits his head on a hard object.

By keeping conflicts on these scripts, murderous violence becomes rare. There is nothing physically stopping one human from hunting another like a deer or butchering one like a lamb. Those blocks are internal—psychological and social.

Do they sometimes fail? Absolutely, and that will be addressed in the appendix on violence.

The scripts are not for individuals, nor are they perfect. The scripts are what have worked through history and prehistory, to get the most people through alive. They work on the average.

Thog and the Lion

> Once upon a time, one of your ancestors was sitting on the savanna with about fifteen other men, women, and children. He had a stick and was poking under a log, hoping to find some ant eggs, when Thog ran out of the brush, screaming. Thog was running as fast as he could for the biggest tree nearby.
>
> Your ancestor ran too. Probably. There's a reason emotions are contagious.
>
> Wugga, widely regarded as the snottiest of the tribe, decided it wouldn't be cool to run. Wugga looked to see what Thog was running from. So the lion killed him first.
>
> MarMar and Roro, young males in the tribe, grabbed sticks and ran toward whatever Thog was running from. They were widely regarded as not very smart but sometimes useful members of the tribe. If they didn't die, they were definitely going to get laid out of it.
>
> That's important, because without either stupid snotty people or stupid aggressive people, the math is bad. Men run and climb faster than women, who run and climb faster than children. Without a few sacrificial males, the women and children die. So dies the tribe and eventually the species.
>
> The stupid brave get breeding rights (hasn't changed much through rescuing the princess and the modern action-adventure movie, has it?) because we will need more stupidly brave people later.

The math is a little clearer on the savanna. The motivations and many of the scripts haven't changed since the dawn of prehistory. Some of it is still valid. We do need people who run toward danger.

But we could do with a few more people like Wugga, who actually look around before they decide to panic. Modern life has fewer circumstances where panic is a bonus. Most of our perceived dangers (cancer, the ecological crisis du jour, international bad guy of the month) give us more than enough time to gather information and make conscious choices.

But the monkey sometimes finds panic far more satisfying.

Your reactions to conflict are for the good of the group.

Section 2.4   Enforcing the Monkey Scripts

Why do we stay on bad scripts?

The first layer of defense is that we rarely see them. They are emotionally triggered and faster than conscious thought. We are often on the script and even finish the script before it occurs to us that we have just done something really stupid.

How many times have you realized something was stupid after you said it? Or not realized it was stupid for hours or days? Or realized those were the same words that got you in trouble in the past? Have you ever looked back over your life and, with a little time and distance, seen patterns of stupid behavior that seemed like habits?

These are scripts. They disguise themselves by seeming rational. That's the second reason we miss them. It's a conversation, right? And you can't have a conversation without thinking, right?

You can though, just as you can have a conversation without listening. It is more accurate to say you can have a conversation with only part of your brain thinking, and that part just reflexively following a script.

> As much as I accept that my monkey and lizard brains are part of me, I dislike scripts because I hate being a puppet, even my own puppet. Once you see the scripts, you can choose to evolve from a meat puppet to an actor, one who acts upon the universe.

The third defense of the scripts is very powerful and very obvious. It is fear of what other people will think. It is also demonstrably, stupidly false.

"Why should I apologize if he's the one being the asshole?" It's a fairly common question. I have heard officers (a very few, it's rare) say they would never apologize to a criminal, and managers say they would never apologize to their employees.

The whole idea is stupid. It is based on a fear of seeming weak or submissive or a parallel fear of being accused of being responsible.

"I'm sorry." Not much as a word thing, huh? Two words, expresses sympathy and nothing else.

Here's the big clue and the monkey trick on this one: "I don't want to apologize because I don't want to look weak." Really? Being afraid of looking weak *denies reality and our own experience.*

We have all seen arguments like this. We have all been part of the audience who will "see the weakness." That's not what happens. We see two people being unreasonable, not one. And the first person to apologize is clearly the smart one, the mature one, the leader. You gain, not lose, status when you make a reasonable, timely, and sincere apology.

From your own experience you have seen this time and again. You know this.

If the other tries to turn it into a sign of weakness, gets so caught up in the monkey dance that he refuses the olive branch or presses for more, the audience identifies him as an ass and he loses status.

We know this from our own experience of being the watchers, the very people you might be afraid to seem weak to. *We know this.* Still, the monkey convinces us to be afraid of what people will think, even though we know they will not think it.

People are not held in check by what people will think. They are held in check by what they *imagine* people will think. That imagination is patently, provably wrong. How much control will you let it have?

Writers and artists talk about the inner critic, the voice in their heads that tells them they will never be good enough and not to even try. It is nothing but the monkey, working to prevent change.

When a young man fights for his girlfriend's honor after a remark or a look, is he driven by what she will think? Does he ask her? Not only do women not see violence the way men do, but women do not see violence the way men think women do.

There are freaks, women who get turned on by violence and will create dangerous drama for the thrill of it. Stay away from them (that advice will not penetrate the brain of anyone who actually needs to hear it, unfortunately). For the most part, that's not the case. To paraphrase the movie *Support Your Local Sheriff*, what a man might think is "yellow" just sounds mature to most women.

This inner critic, with its fear of imaginary censure, is one of the most powerful social controls we have. It is solely responsible for your probably living at the same socioeconomic level you were raised at, not being much more successful than your parents, never finishing that novel or getting your college degree or black belt.

It exists to make sure the group doesn't have to adjust around you, to keep you within your tribe and keep you in your place in your tribe. Is that what you want?

The Inner Critic

I would hazard that almost half of the people reading this are secretly writers or artists. They are working on a book or a screenplay, drawing pictures, or composing music. And almost none will ever send it to a publisher.

What is the voice in your head telling you? It is telling you, "It's not good enough. You will be rejected and embarrassed."

Really?

Here is what happens if you send your novel to a publisher. No, not your novel. If you wrote the worst piece of dreck ever penned in the English language—if you wrote it with crayons on used cocktail napkins—and you sent it in a cardboard box to the biggest publisher in the world, this is what will happen:

You will get a form letter saying, "Thank you for showing us your work. It doesn't fit our needs at this time but we would like to see more when you have it."

How embarrassing is that, really?

If you showed the rejection to your friends, would you get a rush of shame at the failure, or would your friends say, "I never knew you were so creative. Damn. And you sent it out? I'd never be brave enough to do that. Good for you"?

Your status would go up. Your monkey screams the opposite, but we all know it is true.

So what is your monkey really afraid of? It's afraid of the other letter, the one that says, "This is fantastic and we'd like to sign you to a three-book contract with a $100,000 advance and start scheduling your signing tour."

That letter will change your life. And the monkey hates change. But the monkey is clever enough to know, "Don't send it; you might be really successful" is a line not one of us is stupid enough to fall for.

So it tells us the other: That it isn't good enough. That we will be laughed at.

Know this: your own brain will lie to you. It will backstab and sabotage you to prevent *any* change.

There is absolutely nothing wrong with living your life by scripts. They work pretty well pretty often. If you are comfortable and happy and are getting your tasks completed, revel in that.

You are starting to see something now, something that was right in front of you your whole life but invisible. It is easy to overreact and decide something so pervasive and powerful is inherently bad. It isn't. As you learn to see it and control it, you will be able to make things better.

The fourth mechanism that keeps us on scripts is that we excuse them. We explain them. The human brain, with its incredible ability to solve problems, spends most of the time making excuses. You get presented a choice. Your monkey brain chooses while your human brain is still evaluating. Then the monkey brain diverts the human brain into coming up with an explanation of why the choice was good.

> *Decades ago, in an undergraduate psychology course, we were reviewing a study. It was back when left/right brain research was really big. The experimenter brought out a rack of identical shirts, told the subjects they were doing a marketing test, and informed the subjects that all the shirts were from different manufacturers. They then instructed the subjects to pick the best shirt.*
>
> *All the subjects picked a shirt. The experimenters were interested in whether the chosen shirt came from the right or left visual field. What struck me was that in every case, the subjects had an involved, logical explanation of why their chosen (identical) shirt was the best.*

How many times have you seen someone make an obviously stupid decision? In almost every case, the person had a logical-sounding reason. The monkey brain made the bad decision, and the human brain crafted a reason after the fact. Researchers have found they can detect your decisions as much as ten seconds before you are consciously aware of them. (See http://www.nature.com/neuro/journal/v11/n5/abs/nn.2112.html.)

If you are up to a level of self-assessment, think about a time when you did this. If you had been trying to impress a troop of chimps, it's a good bet your monkey-brain reaction would have been the right one.

Section 2.5   Using Your Human Brain

The lizard brain is pretty well adapted to not being eaten by large predators. The monkey brain does fine at handling the social issues inherent in a small, subsistence-level tribe.

Modern life has modern problems. Dealing with policy and law and computers and cars requires the best of our human brains. The modern brain is also well adapted to solving problems with more insight and resources than the monkey or the lizard can bring to the problem. It's a little slow, but it can often solve social conflicts the monkey would prolong, or solve survival problems the lizard would try to endure.

In order to use your human brain, you must learn to

- recognize when you are on a script.
- determine whether the script is helping.
- decide to stay on the script, switch to a different script, or reject scripting altogether.
- check for effect, whichever approach you use.

De-escalate yourself first! Before you can access any communication skills or even think logically, you have to break out of your monkey mind. Scripts frequently ease tension, but no real communication happens on a script.

De-escalate yourself first.

2.5.1 Recognize When You Are on a Script

It will take a lot of practice to avoid scripts altogether, even if that is possible. The scripts trigger themselves faster than conscious thought. You will fall into them. The skill to develop, therefore, is recognizing when this has happened. When you are on a script. When the monkey brain is in charge.

Active listening (see section 3.2) is one way to mitigate the power of your monkey brain. There is nothing inherent in active listening to prevent an emotional reaction or protect your buttons from being pushed. But pausing after listening and before you answer prevents your mouth from going before your brain.

You will get caught in a lot of scripts before you learn to see them from the inside. That's a skill that improves with practice.

These are the signs the monkey is in charge:

- You feel emotion.
- You start to like or dislike the other individual.
- The focus shifts from solving the problem to proving you are right.
- How trumps what.

- You engage in labeling.

- You come up with excuses and justifications.

If **you feel emotion**, you've been hijacked. Anger is a special red flag, because anger is always personal and personal is a monkey-brain thing. But feeling any emotion indicates the limbic system, not the neocortex, is on the job.

This is the scariest concept in the entire program, something I desperately want to be not true: you are physically incapable of making a good decision if you care. If you care, if you feel emotion, if you are passionate about your causes, the part of your brain that makes good decisions is off-line.

There is a reason doctors are not supposed to operate on their own children. Hollywood aside, no detective would be allowed to investigate a sibling's murder. Not just because any defense attorney could get the suspect off, but because surgery and investigations require intelligence and judgment, and emotion hampers those things. It's not so much that emotion makes you stupid as that emotion deactivates the intelligent part of your brain.

You start to like or dislike the individual. Just as the monkey brain is the seat of emotion, it also balances tribal dynamics. That's the primary purpose of social scripts. It doesn't matter whether the feelings are negative or positive ("This guy's being a jerk." Or "Damn, she's cute!"), the monkey issues of status or potential mating or other social concerns have pushed solving the original problem to a back burner.

The focus shifts. There is an old saying in management that you can accomplish almost anything if you don't care who gets credit for it. Everything in this program predicates on the idea that you are interacting with the other person to solve a problem. When the focus shifts from solving the problem to proving you are right, you have stepped into or initiated a pure monkey dominance struggle. As a rule of thumb, if you want the problem solved and don't care who gets credit for it, you are thoroughly in your human brain. The more important credit becomes in that equation, the more influence the monkey is exerting.

When you do access your human brain, this concept becomes an incredibly powerful tool. Want your boss to back your plan? Come up with a solid reason to put her name on it. "You said something at the quarterly meeting that really got me thinking. Want to see what you inspired?"

How trumps what. This is one that is much easier to see in other people than in yourself. When people start defending past practice in the face of better options, they are defending the tribal identity.

There are at least three aspects to this. One is the power of tradition, or simply habit. When I was in, the US Army's dress uniform looked like a cheap business suit from the 1950s. Basketball is played in the underwear of the era in which the game was developed. Changing rules in any sport, even rules designed to prevent injury, is always met with opposition.

Second, since change is always resisted, forcing change is a very common way for new managers to mark territory. Those with strong monkey brains who have been put in an official position of high status but are insecure will be almost driven to prove their power, and one of those ways is change.

The third aspect of "how trumping what" is distracting trivia. One of my friends pointed out that whenever a police agency forms a new specialty team, the first order of business is to design a patch. The amount of effort going into what I call "costumes and jewelry" could have been better spent training.

At a more personal level, I was told once that three of the greatest stressors in a new marriage are

1. whether the toilet paper is rolled from the top or the bottom.

2. whether the toothpaste is squeezed in the middle or rolled up from the bottom.

3. whether presents are opened on Christmas Eve or Christmas morning.

Here's the deal: not one of those things matters. The goal is a happy marriage. The happiness is increased not by winning the battle of the clockwise toilet paper, but in realizing that, compared to a happy marriage, it doesn't matter at all.

You engage in labeling. Labeling and emotion are the two easiest signs to catch in yourself. What is labeling? Labeling is your monkey brain's method of othering people, of putting them in a different tribe. It has the sole purpose of giving you an excuse not to listen to their words. If you try to put the other person in a box, such as, "She's just a secretary," or "What would you expect from a [insert derogatory designator]?" you are labeling that person. Racial slurs and calling someone a racist are exactly the same things for this purpose—it lets your monkey brain pretend this person is not of your tribe and not worthy to have this interaction with you.

You come up with excuses and justifications. This is one I have never caught myself doing in the moment. It sometimes becomes apparent when I read things I wrote long ago or when a friend points it out. We are all members of tribes. We all have our affiliations and memberships, be they our jobs, our political parties, or our sports teams. You will have a tendency to justify what your side does and vilify what the other side does, even if they are doing the same thing.

Long ago, the local paper, on two different pages on the same day, quoted the two presidential candidates. They happened to say the exact same thing, word for word, about each other. The newspaper characterized the words from the candidate they endorsed as "thoughtful and measured" and the exact same words from the other camp as "vicious and unprovoked."

It will be natural for you to make excuses for people with the same identity. That is a huge red flag that you are in your monkey mind on that subject. It might serve you just fine, but don't pretend you are being rational.

In case that's not clear, an example: a close friend wrote extensively about why several of President Bush's policies were very, very wrong. No problem. When President Obama continued some of those policies, the same friend wrote extensively about how those were the best decisions available. Don't get hung up on the example. The *process* is the sign you are looking for.

Recap:

If you are feeling emotion, your limbic system is in charge. This means your neocortex, which could solve the problem, is off-line. You are physically incapable of making a good decision if your monkey brain has been triggered. The part of your brain that makes good decisions is now in the backseat.

Conversely, if you trigger someone else's monkey brain, all the facts, data, and supporting evidence in the world will not help. You have just turned off the part of his brain that cares about things like evidence.

You, like everyone, are physically incapable of making a rational decision if you care, if your emotions get triggered.

If you are feeling for the person, you are balancing social dynamics, not solving problems. The monkey is in charge. Even if the problem is one of social dynamics, your monkey brain will try to re-create the dynamics of a chimp troop, not solve the problem the way your human brain would.

If who gets credit matters, you are not fighting for the project. You are fighting over status, the essential monkey issue.

If you are getting hung up on trivia, you are protecting tribal identifiers.

When you are labeling, othering, depersonalizing, or engaging in any version of "us and them," this has transitioned from problem solving to tribal war. You will sabotage the project and possibly sacrifice yourself for a "win" that exists only in your own head.

"Let me get this straight," the security professional said. "If someone is an asshole by every definition. If everyone who has ever met him in his life thinks, 'What an asshole.' If you made a list of everything an asshole would do and think and say and you could just see all of his behaviors on that list, are you saying he isn't an asshole?"

Not at all. What I am saying is as long as you are calling him an asshole, even in your head, the part of your brain that could manipulate him is turned off. I'm not saying it's not true; I'm saying it's not helpful.

Once you realize you are on a script, what does that mean? It means you are acting subconsciously and may be acting irrationally. You have to evaluate and make a decision.

> Think about the dumbest thing you have ever done. Think about that time when you did or said something so stupid that the second you were committed you knew you would regret it for the rest of your life.
>
> Now, objectively, as little emotion as possible: If you had been trying to impress a troop of chimps, wouldn't the stupid thing have been the right thing to do?
>
> Answer the question and I think you'll see that calling this the monkey brain was no accident. Our instincts are to do things that would impress our tribal ancestors, not our current world.

2.5.2   Is the Script Helping?

The thing with scripts is that we know where most of them end. From the monkey dance in the bar to the argument that ends with make-up sex to the interminable squabble at the board meeting.

Once you realize you are on a script, stop. Take a breath. Recognize it for what it is and decide. Where does this end? Is that where I want it to go?

"Want to go out for dinner tonight?"

"Sure. Where do you want to go?"

"I don't care. Where do you want to go?"

"Doesn't matter to me. You choose."

Sound familiar? With your own spouse or friend or whoever you have the conversation with, you know where it is going to end. In some relationships, it has to go through the cycle a set number of times before the designated person decides. In others, after two cycles, the person who brought up the question will say, "I did see a review for a new restaurant in the paper this morning. That might be fun." It is that predictable.

If the script ends in a good place, you can jump to the end: "Look, you only brought it up because you have something in mind. Why don't you just tell me where we're going?" But that rarely ends well. Remember the monkey brain is comfortable with the script and that means comfort in the relationship. Is causing discomfort worth an extra twenty seconds?

If the script ends in a bad place, you may want do something else.

Mom: "Terry, I got a call from your teacher today. Would you care to explain?"

If the usual script goes through denial and then blaming others and ends at a grounding, Terry may want to try something new.

If the script is helping, let it help. Easing social stress is a big part of what scripts were designed to do.

If it is not helping, if it is sidetracking you from the problem or going somewhere you don't want to go, you will have to make a decision.

2.5.3 Changing or Aborting a Script

There are actually three choices. Many scripts have branches, decision points where you can decide where to take it.

A common thug script is to get angry and loud in an attempt to intimidate. The thug expects one of three reactions because there are three ways the script can commonly go.

The most common is for the thug to be ignored. People stare at the table or the floor, don't meet his eye, and hope not to draw his violent attention. In this case, if he doesn't want anything in particular, like money or rape, he can just feel good about himself by seeing others cower.

Often, someone will try to calm the thug down. If done apologetically and meekly, the thug will usually get a little louder and angrier and often turn it into a low-level mugging. Street hustlers use this tactic, with no direct spoken threat, and it is called "aggressive panhandling." The dynamic is common in schools as well.

If the person trying to calm the thug down doesn't appear meek, the thug will get a little louder to gauge the reaction. If the person who got involved doesn't show concern, the thug will usually back off with a few insults as he leaves.

The third permutation of the script is for someone to get loud and aggressive back at the thug. That leads to a straight monkey-dance scenario.

One starting point, three common scripts. All have predictable endings.

So the first question to ask yourself, if you have recognized you are on a script and don't like where it ends: Is there an opportunity to push it toward another version of the script with a better ending?

The second option is to choose another script entirely. Each script has roles. Sometimes the roles are similar—the players in a monkey dance are interchangeable. Usually, though, there are differences.

A common romantic script is the rescue. One person has a horrible past of abuse and betrayal and latches on to a romantic partner who wants to be the hero and protect her from all badness.

The protection from harm quickly becomes a protection from consequences. The rescued princess uses the relationship as a safe environment where growth and becoming strong are not necessary. The relationship quickly becomes codependent. The victim cannot survive on her own, and the rescuer gets his identity from shielding her from the world.

The script is common. It is extremely dysfunctional. One counterscript when approached by the maiden in distress is the mentor: "I don't want a relationship, but I will teach you how to be strong."

The interesting thing about this counterscript is that most of the time it is rejected. The princess has no desire to be strong herself but just wants to be continuously rescued.

Rejecting the script is as simple as ignoring the damsel in distress and walking away. Or offering to find help. My favorite is to say, "My wife is really good at giving advice on stuff like this. Let me introduce you."

Scripts have roles. The role is not about individuals. A teacher teaches students. When someone is in the teacher role, someone else must be in the student role. It doesn't matter who. If the students do not appear, the teacher must transition to another role—perhaps mother or father or friend. If potential students are there, the teacher may try to force people to play the student role.

In none of this is the identity of either player important. To play out the teacher/student script requires a *student*, not Jimmy Smith, not me, not you. Any individual capable of filling the role will do.

A boss cannot be a boss without subordinates. A criminal cannot be a criminal without victims. *Qualities* are important. A victim should be meek, unaware, and have something worth taking. As long as these qualities are present, who the victim is (name, identity, other factors of personality) are irrelevant.

This information is critical because our instincts and training are to assume that when a conflict gets heated, the situation is personal. It will feel personal. It can potentially escalate to a dangerous rage. It is not personal. That is something your monkey brain needs to believe.

If you can grasp this, and understand that the person is stuck in a script, it can help you stay calm enough to step out of yours.

It also introduces a tactic. There are a great number of roles, archetypes, and stereotypes, any of which can perform in a script. Each has shadings and nuance. As a teacher, I can be a guide, a mentor, or a lecturer. When someone assumes a teaching role expecting me to play student, I can choose to play colleague or fellow explorer or devil's advocate.

When someone engages you in conflict, you can fight back and step into the monkey dance. Or you can choose: how would I handle this as a drill sergeant? As a chaplain? As a parent? As a willing victim? As a reluctant victim? Each of these roles will lend itself to a new script with a different ending.

As an officer dealing with difficult inmates, part of my job was to control their behavior. I could do so as an authority figure, an enemy, a fellow human . . . the options were infinite. Frequently, I would ask myself, "If I liked this kid, how would I phrase it?"

This tactic is incredibly difficult for most people. We lock into our identity and don't want to change. We feel it is not a real win if we win by being someone else.

Unless part of your personal identity definition is "actor," you will likely eschew this incredibly powerful tactic. Tell me, is that a rational decision or your monkey brain?

As an experiment, if you have a running argument or disagreement with someone, the next time it flares up, resolve not to be you. Hold the conversation as if you were a friend or an uncle or Mother Theresa. Anybody but you. See how the script changes.

To abort a script, you must step off the script completely. This is hard to do. Not only are the scripts subconscious and hard to see, but they follow patterns to the end. When you do not finish a script, you will often be left with a vague unsatisfied sense that something is wrong— like you left the stove on at home. This is what we call the "unfinished business feeling." It will likely affect not only you, but the other people involved in the script.

Remember always that you are going for a human-level win. The assumptions throughout this book are that you have a job to do and problems to solve, and the conflict scripts are interfering with that goal.

If your goal is the dominance game or appeasing your monkey issues or someone else's, then aborting a script will rarely help.

To abort the script you focus on the problem and acknowledge the monkey trap. You do not play the monkey game:

"Who sent you to do the schedule? That's my job!"

"Let's figure out why the chief assigned me later. Right now, who do we put in the B pod?"

This is hard because the monkey brain wants to complete the script and our lifetime of social conditioning makes it easy.

In *Meditations on Violence* there is an essay entitled "Permission." I wrote that a potential victim must give him- or herself permission to be rude. What I meant, though we hadn't worked out the concepts yet, was in order to avoid victimization, a target must be able to break social conventions. Must be able to step off the scripts. The predators count on the victims' staying scripted and predictable.

Marc MacYoung, codesigner of this program, rightly pointed out that a certain percentage of people would read that they must be rude and interpret it as "they must be assholes."

Here's the deal. Assholes are extremely predictable. There is no surer sign you are on a script than predictability. It is very, very easy to believe you are stepping off script while just going into a different script.

2.5.4 Check for Effect

Do not get complacent when you have shifted or gotten off the script. In general, if you get off the script, the other person's monkey brain has no idea what to do and the human brain must step up. That's the goal, to get people thinking instead of following scripts.

But in some people, especially if they find the situation threatening, the absence of a script will increase the fear. They may become more dangerous, more unpredictable. It's rare, but it does happen.

In all things, not just in conflict communications but in every aspect of your life, check for effect. Periodically pause and evaluate whether your strategies are working. Is the person getting calmer? If not, this is the wrong tactic for getting her calm.

Everything in life. If your career isn't progressing, something needs to change. What you are doing now is not working. Health. Relationships.

Check for effect and adjust your tactics as necessary.

Section 2.6 Staying at the Human Level

This is not about making your human brain so strong that it can control your limbic system. No simple handbook can beat that much evolution. This is about two things: preventing other people from getting into their monkey brains, or, if it is too late, appeasing the limbic system so you can engage with their human brains and, first and foremost, appeasing your monkey brain so it shuts up and lets the humans talk.

2.6.1 You vs. "Ya"

Note: This section may be specific to American English. Everything else in the program has been taught, tested, and given accolades in Hungarian, Slovenian, Spanish, and German.

Have you noticed that you almost never use the full form of the word "you" in conversations with friends?

"How ya doin'?"

"Whatcha up to?"

"How are you doing?" aloud, feels accusatory.

"You" becomes a very powerful word in scripts. It makes things feel personal, makes it seem that this is a battle of wills between two individuals and our very selves are riding on it. That's simply not true.

From the monkey dance step of "What are you lookin' at?" to a handcuffed arrestee calling the officer a "pussed-up piece of shit," they are insults designed to hurt—but they aren't personal.

The monkey dancer responds to the situation and possibly misinterprets a stray look as a challenging stare. He doesn't know or care anything about the individual. It is not personal. The criminal does not know anything about the officer. His behaviors and words are reactions to the uniform and the situation. The actual individual is almost irrelevant to the situation. The script merely requires roles.

"You" sucks us in. "You" makes us feel the insult or the threat is aimed at us. "You" can snatch us completely out of our human minds.

There may be a problem that requires logic and clear thinking, human-brain stuff. The idea that "you" is personal is carefully cultivated by the monkey brain. The minute it hears the word "you," the monkey brain says, "Take a backseat, logic. This is getting personal and it's my area of expertise."

The monkey brain steps into control.

The first thing the monkey does is use the word "you" right back. If they weren't before, now all involved are in their monkey brains. The monkey is satisfied. It likes it there and it is much easier to deal with another monkey rather than a human. The actual problem never gets solved, but the monkey doesn't really care about deadlines and the like.

The challenge is not to use the "you" back, to stay in our human minds. It can be difficult. Our language is set up to use that word a lot.

"What's your problem?" is obvious. It gets read automatically as a challenge. But the variations invite conflict scripts as well.

"Why are you angry?" invites defensiveness: *I'm not angry. How dare you presume to tell me what I think or feel?*

Even the weasel-words variations, "You look angry" or "I get the sense that you're upset" invite justifications and explanations, merely defensiveness lite.

"What are you doing?" invites justification and explanation. It is automatically taken as some kind of accusation. There is no way to say it, no syllable that can be emphasized that won't read as an accusation.

This power of "you" is so endemic to the language that if we actually want to know what someone is doing, just get the information, we deliberately and universally garble the words: "Watcha doin'?" The "you" fades to the background.

Another alternative, "What's going on?" can be heard as a request for information or as an accusation, depending on context and emphasis. There is no "you" in that sentence.

To avoid the script, you must acknowledge the monkey trap without poking at it. Drop "you." It's a challenge. This will be addressed later, in a section on tactics, but as much as possible without seeming insincere or stilted, use the word "we." It's still tribal, but helps to prevent othering and encourage cooperation.

2.6.2 Don't Take It Personally

What does that even mean? In Conflict Communications the meaning is very specific. It takes history to hate a person. There must be a history of wrongs or perceived wrongs in order to get a deep and personal emotional bond, positive or negative.

Love at first sight? It's a hormone reaction. Sometimes it grows into something deeper and it might be fun to fantasize about the stranger who met your eye and smiled all those years ago—but love, friendship, and even hate take time and contact.

Rage doesn't. Nor does infatuation. Those can be triggered in the monkey brain by scripts.

> *The script has been playing for a long time. Things went really well, especially early in the relationship. She was everything he dreamed: pretty, smart, and devoted. It got rocky later. "Smart" meant she kept telling him what to do. If she'd just listened when he told her to stop, things would have been perfect.*
>
> *But she didn't listen. She said he wasn't the boss. She knew he was bigger and stronger but didn't think that should matter. It did matter. He tried to tell her. She just did whatever she wanted anyway. The first time he pushed her, she screamed at him and actually hit him. So he hit her back. Not hard. A slap. Nothing really.*
>
> *For the next couple of days she was quiet, almost meek. He felt bad so he got her some flowers, took her to dinner. Paid her a lot of attention. She liked that, but it was a long time before she started trying to boss him around. That ended the same way.*
>
> *Now, usually, all he has to do is give her the look and she's meek again. Usually. Sometimes it takes a little more to get her attention. That's where things were when the busybody stranger stuck his nose in their business and tried to get him to stop.*
>
> *Stranger had to be taught to mind his own business. He got what was coming to him.*

The narrator in this story—does he hate the woman he abuses? Not in his mind. He is maintaining control. He is on a script, perfectly comfortable in his monkey mind.

Does he hate the stranger he teaches a lesson to? The beating was probably savage; it often is when an outsider gets involved in an in-group dispute. Does he hate the stranger? It's a rage, but again it comes from the script. That savage beating is not much different than captured soldiers getting mutilated or gruesome medieval executions. It is just a reaction to outsiders. Sending a signal.

"Don't take it personally" means this: if there is no history, if you do not know the person or if you do but there has been no history of harm or betrayal, it is not personal. The person may try to make it seem personal, to satisfy both your monkey brain and his or hers, but it isn't.

This understanding helps to give you the option of staying calm and dealing with the human-level problem.

It works the other way as well. If you dislike someone or start to feel anger and irritation, take a breath and check yourself. Do you have history with this person? Have you harmed or been harmed by this person? If there was harm, was it based on the circumstances?

> *When interviewing for the tactical team, one candidate failed twice. In each interview we had two scenarios. The candidates probably believed we were testing tactical knowledge. We weren't. In each of the scenarios was a fundamental decision point that hinged on character.*
>
> *One was whether the person would be blindly obedient. These were high-end operators who would be called in to ugly situations and needed to adapt independently. I needed people who would tell me when I was wrong and refuse an order if the situation in front of them warranted it. We neither needed nor wanted obedient sheep on this team.*
>
> *The second scenario tested a different character issue.*
>
> *The candidate failed twice, both times on the scenario. In many ways he would have made a good operator—fit, intelligent, caring—but he assumed making me happy, following my orders, was a higher priority than it was.*
>
> *He assumed, since I had given the scenarios in both of his interviews, that I disliked him. That it was personal.*

If previous loss, injury, or problems can be explained by circumstance (an interview as above or a legitimate business rivalry or coincidence), assume that. There is an old saying, "Never ascribe to malice what can better be explained by stupidity." That's good advice.

That said, you can take it too far. Adultery is clearly an issue with monkey-based territory and group-preservation connotations. Don't assume that just because you think it was reasonable, the wronged spouses will agree.

Which brings up two important things:

1. Your monkey brain is sneaky and powerful. This book is written with the intention of giving your human brain an edge. Unfortunately, it is also giving you an entirely new monkey trap. When you start feeling superior because you see the scripts and others don't, that's your monkey brain. When you start using the concepts of "It's only an abstraction, just my monkey brain trying to get in the way" to do things that you know are wrong, that's your monkey brain jockeying for power.

2. Breaking rules. Whether the scripts are based on ancient ways of living that no longer exist or not, the scripts have given us a set of rules that allow us to live together in relative harmony. There is a qualitative difference between silencing the inner voice that is holding you back and encouraging someone else to take drugs to be part of a group. There is a difference between aborting a script to get to the real problem and violating a social taboo. Most of the monkey scripts work to keep us living together. Do not violate territoriality or break a taboo and expect to avoid consequences through reasoning.

2.6.3   Reality, Unreality, and the Shadow Community

There's a concept that must be explained and it is very difficult to do with the written word. Let's start with reality maps.

None of us deals with the world as it is. We have a map or a model of how we think the world works. We think, act, and feel based on that map. It is not true. If we are honest, it is just the best working model we have right now. If we never challenge it, our model becomes the truth, and our monkey minds will defend it to the death.

Truth is not relative. Only zero is zero. One is closer to zero than twenty-six, but only zero is zero. Some reality maps are very accurate. Sometimes big insights can shift our reality maps toward much greater accuracy, but no level of insight can make our beliefs about life into life.

Within this concept, we all have beliefs and expectations. Voices in our heads that tell us what is right and what is wrong, that advise us about how others will perceive our actions. Often these voices are wildly inaccurate.

We've already mentioned the resistance to apology: the voices in our heads make us think we will seem weak or deserve blame. The voice is there even though we know from personal experience that we see an apology as an act of maturity and leadership. We know this if we think about it. We still hear, and all too often heed, the voices.

> The young man was considering breaking up with his girlfriend. He loved her, and liked her, and admired her. It was a strong relationship and he had been happy, but he was considering breaking it off because he was sure she was about to leave him, and he didn't think he could take that.
>
> A few months before, you see, he and his lady had gone for a long walk on a deserted beach and had run into a group of young men. The men were drunk and getting rowdy. There were a half dozen or so. They saw the young man and the woman and started saying some pretty inappropriate things. It looked like it had the potential to get ugly.
>
> The young man apologized, acted deferential, and got out of there with his girlfriend, as fast as he could.

Author's note: That was a damn good decision. Young drunk males in a pack, no witnesses, one male and one female as potential victims—the stage was set for a potential rape and murder or murders. There was no good possible outcome from staying.

> *The young man asked for advice. His reasoning was that no woman that wonderful could stand to stay with a man who was a coward, one who wouldn't "stand up for her honor" and fight when she was insulted.*
>
> *I advised him to talk to her. I told him women did not see these things the way men did.*
>
> *He talked to her and was surprised. She barely remembered the incident that had been eating at him. Her only thought concerning his cowardice or manhood was a sense of gratitude that she was lucky enough to be with a man who "wasn't stupid."*

It's not just that women don't think about violence and conflict the way men do. Women don't think the way men believe women do. Read that again. It's a big clue.

The shadow community we have in our heads, the voices telling us what other people believe and think, aren't accurate. The voices are powerful, certainly. That doesn't make them right.

When we listen to the voices, we are not being logical or thoughtful. We are listening to conditioning that pertained to conditions on the savanna twenty thousand years ago.

On the other end, less primitive, is the concept of idealism.

I've been trying to avoid politics throughout the book. Though the world of politics is thick with excellent examples of monkey-brain thinking, many if not most of the readers will have tribal identity built into their political beliefs. Bringing up politics will almost automatically turn off the neocortex, and I'd rather avoid that. For this book to work, I need you thinking.

In my lifetime, I remember eight presidents. Some I liked, one I despised, but none of them really affected my life much. That, in the end, was their job. To continue and maintain this concept of "America." To that end, they were all successful. Despite dire predictions of power plays and martial law, even the one contested election resulted in a peaceful transfer of power.

Many things have changed, but America is still America. Bill Gates and Steve Jobs have done much more to change my day-to-day life than any president. Which means the presidents have done what they were elected to do.

How they did their jobs, where they put their priorities . . . that is open to endless debate.

Here's the deal: we all have a vision of America. Whether an individual considers a president good or bad is based not on how the president did, but on how closely his methods matched our individual ideals. All presidents preserved the union. Not all did it in the way we believe "America should act."

That "should"—those beliefs and ideals—are part of our map. They are not real. Like any other value, they do not exist outside of our heads. But they are ripe for tribalism and the monkey brain.

The departure into politics was because it is universal. All of the readers of any country can go back over their own experience and see who preserved or failed to preserve a nation (which is objective) and see that it has little to do with likes and dislikes. Abraham Lincoln, arguably our greatest president, is the one who came closest to losing the Union. Who we like and dislike (when we do not know the person, as is common in politics and big business and other things) is based on our perception of how closely they mirrored our ideals.

It is still tribal thinking, and has a huge potential to cause conflict. But I can't help but think a tribe based on ideals instead of blood or geography has huge potential. The human mind and the monkey mind, working together, can be the idealist.

The monkey brain does not distinguish between ideas and reality. "The name is the thing" was an ancient belief in both religion and magic. Aristotle's *Metaphysics* was the first real attempt to distinguish that what something is *called* isn't what it *is*.

Symbols are powerful, but on some level your brain thinks that the symbol is the thing. That a needle stuck in a doll actually stabs the person the doll represents. That the words you hear or see have their own truth. This level of the brain is the part that allows hypnotism to happen.

In some cases being told, "You don't feel pain" is as effective as anesthesia to remove pain. People can be convinced that water is colder or hotter than it is. Or that cheese mold that looks like Jesus can heal.

These are silly ideas. But that is your monkey brain. The word "silly" is the clue. It is a way to other, to say the people who believe this are less than you. Your tribe would never believe something so foolish. To believe may be monkey brain. But so is mocking those beliefs.

You do believe things like this. Many of our big abstract ideas are just words. There is nothing there we can put in a wheelbarrow.

If you are a patriot, willing to lay down your life for America, what is "America"? The geographical borders? Those have changed vastly since the original thirteen states. All of the people in those borders? I've met some of the worst and would really rather not die for some of 'em. The ideals of America? Which ideals? Those laid out originally in the Constitution? Or those practiced in Congress today? Or those ideals exemplified by television commercials?

It is a vague idea, really just a symbol of something we can't quite define, but many people, including me, have taken oaths to defend it even to the death.

The same with ideals like "social justice." *Liberté, égalité, fraternité.* Equality and liberty can't even coexist without a lot of mental gymnastics or some new definitions of the words. Freedom to excel means, by definition, that some will excel and some won't . . . and equality is gone.

These ideals, these words have created huge social changes. Many of the surviving changes have been positive, but some of the worst crimes and genocides and wars in modern history have been likewise spurred by ideals: over twenty million executed to ensure a worker's paradise that failed; possibly fifty million total in World War II, fought against the ideal of National Socialism.

Even down to modern crime and gangs who kill over "turf" and colors—which are largely symbols for the very real deeper reason of market share in the drug culture. But market share is too abstract. The human brain grasps the idea; the monkey does not. The pure human brain rarely kills, and when it does, it is dispassionate.

That may seem like a digression, but this is critical. When we write that your subconscious scripts are for the "good of the group," you must understand that the group is not the collection of individuals who compose the group. It is the *idea* of the group. For that matter, the group may only exist in the mind at all (as in obsessed stalkers).

When an abuser attacks a spouse, the abuser damages his own soul, the victim's body, and the psyches of the children. It is an act of profound damage to every single member of the family. The monkey brain and the script in particular serves the idea of "family." It is for the good of "preserving the family."

And the horrible thing is that the monkey brain is right. If the victim does the intelligent thing and takes the kids and leaves, the family has died. Which was what the monkey feared all along. All of the monkeys, including the kids, including the victim, want the beating to end. They don't want the family to end. The monkey scripts act to preserve the group.

And the monkey brain is powerful. It takes an extreme act of will, or the lizard waking up, to change the scripts.

Section 2.7   Hooks

Dealing with people who routinely used violence to get what they want, they often sought a "hook." A hook is an excuse to act out or a rationalization that will allow them to excuse their actions later.

In the extreme, a career criminal who violently beat a teenage girl doesn't get a lot of social status with his peer group for a random beating. "The bitch told me to fuck off so I had to teach her a lesson," plays much better with his buddies.

Hooks are not the reasons for acting out. They are excuses. Nor are they limited to escalating situations to violence. Administrators who feel a need to chew out someone will actively seek excuses, poring through reports for minor errors so they have an ostensible reason for doing what they were going to do anyway.

Understand that dynamic. The motivation to act out comes first. Then the hook is sought. Then the bad behavior happens.

The motivation can come from a number of sources. With criminals, the most common motivation for robbery is to get money for drugs. But it satisfies the monkey mind if there is a better excuse, something that comes from somewhere higher on Maslow's hierarchy than fear of withdrawals. The most egregious (and funniest, to my mind) was a famous prisoner who described his early armed robberies as his Maoist prerevolutionary phase.

Hooks also help to other the victim, which frees the criminal to use more force.

In less extreme examples, a person who is suddenly feeling insecure about his or her dominance or place in the hierarchy may feel a need to act out and dominate subordinates. This is pure monkey stuff, and in the criminal subculture the dynamic is the same. A tough guy who feels he has been humiliated is likely to beat someone else to "get his manhood back." The person he beats may have nothing to do with the humiliation and will almost certainly be someone he can easily and safely dominate, perhaps his child or significant other. He will, however, seek a hook to justify it, exactly the same as a boss will.

The hook (in a criminal scenario) hinges on getting you to say or do something that can be considered an insult.

The mental gymnastics involved in this can be pretty extreme. The person who starts off the conversation with, "What you lookin' at, cocksucker?" will find nothing wrong with his own words but will take, "Screw you. Leave me alone" as a deadly insult.

The key to not giving away hooks begins with an ability to show elaborately relaxed body language. That can be very hard. The monkey does not distinguish between humiliation and death, or between a verbal social challenge and a hungry tiger. Your adrenaline, unless you have a lot of experience with this, will likely shoot through the roof. It will be hard to keep your voice steady, not shake visibly, and keep a steady gaze.

If you can, you treat the challenges as thoughtful questions, acting like you didn't hear the personal insults:

"What you lookin' at, cocksucker?"

"Hm? Just zoning out. Had a long day. How ya doin'?"

"What the fuck do you mean by that?"

It's hard not to get insulting or sarcastic here. That's the monkey trap. He couldn't understand a simple question, so he must be the stupid monkey—you're much smarter—but he wants you to act superior as an excuse to hurt you.

Don't ignore or denigrate your own question either. "I didn't mean anything" sounds defensive. The key to making this work is based on animal psychology. Remember dominance games and the monkey dance? There are divisions as well. Lions do not get into dominance games with cheetahs. Adult dogs do not get into dominance games with puppies. The adult remains cool, aloof, and above it. To make this tactic work you must be and stay above the emotional landscape.

"I meant I was tired. Asked how things were going with you. Yeah."

Handled at the right level it is hard for someone searching for hooks to keep up steam. He pushes too far and it backfires—witnesses know he was being the asshole. He will likely walk away muttering an insult. You pretend not to notice. Nor do you smile or look smug. The essence of the big-dog tactic is to show that this whole incident was beneath your notice.

If you respond to the muttered insult, or look around with a grin to see who admired your deft handling, or just look smug, the aggressor knows he has been played and you have just handed him a hook.

In a potentially violent situation after you win, keep your mouth shut. Your monkey wants to brag. Assume the situation is not over.

If the threat doesn't leave and pushes ("You trying to be funny?"), there are two options for de-escalating without resorting to force.

The first option is to leave. "I have an appointment. I'm leaving." Or, occasionally, "I don't like where this is going. I'll just leave." In neither of these, especially the latter, should there be any emotion in your voice. At this point, you leave. Ideally, you will turn your back on the threat while keeping him in your view.[1] The threat may still insult or challenge. Ignore it. Especially fight the urge to get in the last word as you cross the threshold. The monkey really wants to get that last word in.

---

[1] How is this possible, you ask with innocent, wide eyes? That's what shadows and reflections are for. If you're really good, you can watch the other people in a room and tell almost exactly what the bad guy is doing.

The second option is to raise the stakes. I don't recommend this unless you really know how to handle yourself around criminals and violence. It is very, very effective at preventing violence, but if it fails, it has the potential to fail catastrophically. Bluffing with criminals is ill advised. They have far more experience at bluffing citizens than citizens do at bluffing criminals.

In raising the stakes, you address the behavior directly. You must still remain calm and detached, or at least sound and look calm and detached. "Why are you trying to make me angry?" is one tactic. I've extensively used "What's your goal here, partner?" Once (and it was funny), I said, "I just realized you're trying to hurt my feelings. How bad would you feel if you made me cry?" The effectiveness of that one had a lot to do with the fact that it was coming from an experienced jail guard.

Addressing the behavior directly and remaining calm and unemotional sends a very specific message to the aggressor: you know exactly what he is doing and you are both prepared for and experienced in dealing with bad things. It sends the message that what he wants (a fight, to hurt someone) will have a very high price tag. If he is concerned about overcoming a humiliation, he will be very reluctant to risk losing.

The stakes are high for you in this as well. Do not bluff this tactic.

In a nonviolent setting, the tactics are the same. When someone wants to vent or show who is boss in a meeting or negotiation, the tactics are the same, minus (usually) the profanity.

"Explain to me what the hell you were thinking when you wrote *this* in the report."

If you get defensive—and you will want to—it is monkey brain to monkey brain. A dominance game and an excuse to chew you out, the corporate equivalent of a beatdown. Answer as if it were a thoughtful, reasoned question.

Whether the person you are dealing with is playing a monkey dominance game or is a pure predator, he wants to deal with a monkey. When you are in your monkey brain, you are emotional and most of all *predictable*. Predators (rapists, robbers, murderers—but also the cold-blooded corporate ladder climber) thrive on this and count on you following your social scripts.

No one with bad intentions, whether those intentions are social or asocial, wants to deal with you in your human brain. The human brain plans. The human brain comes up with solutions to problems and antagonistic people thrive on problems.

Neither wants to deal with your lizard brain, should it awaken—a perfectly ruthless animal machine that only cares about your survival.

The monkey is the safest to prey on, the safest to challenge and humiliate. Anyone who wishes to take advantage of you wants you in your monkey brain. And your monkey wants to be there too.

If you get hooked, you will find yourself on a script. If you get angry, if you start labeling, if you want to show who is best—you know the signs. You must recognize it and then spit out the hook.

Take a deep breath. Acknowledge your internal state. Get back to the problem.

Deep breath. "Sorry, I was starting to get angry for some reason. So what should we do about the situation in building C?"

It acknowledges the monkey trap but refuses to play. Does not make it personal (no "you" in there) and focuses back on the problem. It even uses "we" as a way to build a perceived unity.

Breaking Out of the Monkey Brain

Step 1. Recognize when you have been hijacked. Emotion? Labeling? (See section 2.5.1.)

Step 2. Do not deny it.

Step 3. Take a deep breath.

Step 4. Say, out loud, "Sorry about that. I was starting to get emotional for some reason. What were we working on?" Change that last sentence to suit.

It is that simple.

Everything in this book reverses, sometimes on many levels. Monitor yourself. Once you have practiced, it is easy to see when people are looking for hooks. It is harder to identify when *we* are looking for hooks.

When you get angry or off balance, even for stupid reasons, like sleep deprivation, you might start looking for hooks. Anger works as a source of quick energy and enthusiasm, but we are conditioned that we need something or someone to be angry at. So we start looking for hooks.

Many negative scripts start by looking for a hook. Be as honest as you can (it can be very difficult to honestly self-evaluate). The last time you argued with your teenager over homework, did you discover the homework wasn't done and get angry? Or were you feeling slightly grumpy and then asked about the homework?

On one level or another, we all look for hooks. Just be aware.

There are automatic, natural hooks. Some can't be helped. If you wear a uniform to work or if you are of a visibly different group than the people around you, you are automatically othered to some extent. That othering is an automatic hook for those who want to act out.

The key to minimizing this effect is to work from the common ground. I found out long ago that arguing with schizophrenics about what they see is a waste of time. "I know you see the blue people and you know I can't see them, so let's talk about what we both see," was a great tactic to get people to open up.

The same idea works cross-culturally. Before you even consider talking about social, political, or value differences, spend a lot of time on common ground. Almost everybody loves his or her family. In Iraq I'd often start by talking about how much I loved the food. Even if I wasn't a believer, I'd read the Koran, at least a translation, and had enough knowledge in common to know that a translation didn't really count.

Find the common ground and then be sure to listen more than you talk.

Your other natural hooks may well be under your control. You might well be an ass. If people regularly dislike you "for no reason," there is a reason and it is you.

Being rude is an automatic hook. Being cruel or insensitive are automatic hooks. If your language is filled with racist or sexist terms, even if you think it is funny, you are giving away hooks.

And in some environments, talking like an overly educated, holier-than-thou reformer is an automatic hook. Don't get any tribal feelings about that description either. The most sanctimonious holier-than-thou people I know are progressive social activists, not religious zealots. (Ooooh. Look at all the labeling in that sentence!)

You can't directly see your sanctimoniousness, or your rudeness, or when you are being an ass. Maybe you can, actually, but most people don't look that hard. Look, instead, for the way people treat you.

If they avoid you, you're probably an ass. If you can only have conversations on certain subjects with people who share your point of view, you're probably a sanctimonious prick.

Monitor yourself for the hooks you give away and ruthlessly cut them out of your language and demeanor. Unless you thrive on meaningless conflict. In that case, do whatever you want.

Last thing: There is a universal way to see who you are, if you have the courage. You are reflected in your friends. If you have no friends, or all of your friends are asses, it's you. You're an ass. Hate to be the one to tell you.

If, on the other hand, you look at your friends and feel humble that people so cool are willing to spend time with you, in that case you are doing well. Just don't get smug.

Section 2.8   The Monkey Problem

I tell people that being a corrections officer is a safe, easy job for intelligent people who pay attention. It is a very difficult, very dangerous job for stupid people and those who don't pay attention.

The essence is in what the officer wants—a clean, quiet, safe environment. The prisoners want the same things. It's true that no one likes being told he is making things dirty or loud or unsafe, but even the prisoners who feel entitled to endanger others also want to feel safe.

If the officers and the inmates want the same thing, how does it turn into a battle?

It's the same in every environment. In a family, all the people want a safe harbor, love and respect, a group of mutual caring. In a business the purpose is profit and no one goes to work hoping for stress and friction and a miserable eight hours. No one wakes up in the morning and thinks, "You know, I'm going to do a real shitty job today. I'm going to make sure my workplace is less safe and all my coworkers hate me."

And yet in environments from family to prison, there is friction and sometimes every day is a battle.

Why? Because there are multiple layers to everything and what we want as people may not be what we want as monkeys.

All the lizard cares about is survival. It's involved in other things—movement, music—but even sex, one of the things your animal self should own, has become so tied with ideas about image and value and esteem that the monkey has taken it over.

So the lizard doesn't come into a lot of conflict. Most of the conflict surrounding you is just meaningless chattering to the lizard. If the lizard awakes, the stakes have become very high and it can be a game changer. Sometimes it will freeze you. Your lizard's millennia of dealing with predators will not let you move even when your training says you must move or die. Training, to the lizard, is an abstraction and not real, not until the lizard sees it work.

Sometimes the lizard will explode you into action, make you or let you do things you didn't believe were possible. No matter what happens, the lizard, when it wakes, changes things.

In our society very few people will ever get involved in a conflict at the lizard level. That's a good thing.

The human part of the brain deals with the problem. Whether it is getting your daily report in or arranging to move large masses of material and personnel to a disaster site, people often come together to solve problems.

Solving problems in most cases should be easy: identify the problem, prioritize a plan, list necessary resources, gather resources, execute the plan. As long as both people are working from their human brains there is very rarely a conflict, and when conflict does arise, it can be resolved rationally and respectfully.

In actual application, it is almost never easy. Things become personal. Conflicts arise. People start acting like people.

The real conflicts are almost never over the problem. They are over status or credit or identity or protocols.

When you are trying to deal with a problem and others are dealing with personalities, ask yourself: "What's the monkey problem?"

2.8.1   Categories of Monkey Problems

We have identified six categories of monkey problems. Only six. All related to status, territory, or protocols.

Status Checking
Dominance
We Don't Do That Here
You Don't Belong Here
Snowflakes
Untouchables

Once upon a time, my bosses issued a memo to be read at briefings. The memo informed the line staff at the sheriff's office that we were facing a budget crisis, that the management team was working very hard to ensure that the impact on services and personnel would be minimal, but that the deputies at the bottom of the seniority list might want to make some contingency plans.

You don't send a memo like that to four hundred problem solvers without getting solutions. I took a look and thought, "Cool. I know where we can save a half million dollars."

Because this wasn't my area of expertise (I was CERT leader at the time and working mental health units), I did some research, crunched some numbers, studied proposal format, and put together a tight, irrefutable package.

I then picked the administrator I most admired to take the proposal to. He'd been an outstanding sergeant and lieutenant and had recently made captain, a level at which he could potentially make policy changes. I wanted this proposal to go to him to do anything I could to give his a career a boost.

I dressed up, made an appointment, walked in.

The meeting was a disaster. I had triggered four different monkey problems in one smooth move.

1. **Status checking.** When a new dog comes around, all the other dogs have to sniff butts. This is how they identify who the dog is. It's no different for people.

When you get a great idea that will save your organization a huge amount of money and take it to the right person, more often than not nothing will happen. There will be a friendly discussion and promises to look at it. Lots of questions about how you are doing. You feel vaguely blown off. It can cause bitterness.

When you come into any situation as an unknown quantity—a new student or employee, a transfer, or just someone with an idea that fits outside of his or her job description—the monkey demands that the *unknown quantity problem* be addressed first. We must know, but especially people in established power positions in a hierarchy are compelled to know, who you are and where you fit. That problem must be solved before the human problem can ever be considered.

Are you trying to get recognition? To climb the ladder? To make management look bad?

It will be discussed later, but the primary goal of the people you are likely to take a solution to is *not* to solve the day-to-day problems of the organization. It is not to do things better or more efficiently or to safeguard the feelings of staff. It isn't even to live up to, much less enforce, the company's vision and mission statements. Their job is to preserve and maintain the organization into the future.

A potential shake-up in status, which you represent as an unknown quantity, endangers that primary mission.

When I took that proposal to the captain's office, I was a tactical guy offering a budget solution. I might as well have been a talking seal.

2. **Dominance.** In any group, someone will be in charge. In a well-run, mission-oriented group, that leadership will shift depending on the needs of the situation. In a laidback recreational group, the leadership will be light.

In many groups, not only will there be a leader, but there will be people vying for leadership *and* a strict hierarchy. Wherever you are, except for the top and the bottom, you will have one person directly above you and a specific number directly below.

The more secure everyone is in this hierarchy the less likely that serious conflicts erupt. Young children are comforted with parents making decisions. They are not, in most cases, constantly striving to be the boss of the family.

An uncertain hierarchy—where roles are not clearly defined or where a big boss with a lot of power can play favorites by whim, or a new group without an established pecking order—are ripe for conflict.

Anything that threatens status triggers the monkey. I was bringing a solution to someone I admired and valued as a friend. I had interpreted the memo as a cry for help (as had the rest of the line staff) and was trying to help. The captain, unfortunately, could only interpret my solution as a challenge to his authority. By helping him with his job, he was hearing that he couldn't do his job. I had challenged his status and his monkey brain needed to prove he was in charge—by not accepting the help.

3. **We don't do that here.** Every group has rules and protocols. In many groups, these rules are unofficial. That does not mean they are not enforced.

There may be an official open-door policy with the big boss, but using it may be a violation of the protocol to use the chain of command. These unwritten rules may cover who talks to whom and what subjects are off limits in certain areas and which reports it is OK to ignore.

I jumped the chain of command with my proposal. Broke a protocol.

4. **You don't belong here.** In some organizations, there are subgroups with strong tribal identities. They jealously guard their territory, which may be physical ("What are you doing in officer country, Private?") or may be more symbolic ("Don't tell me you tried installing software yourself").

You may be working in the same company or going to the same school. That does not mean you belong in the same world. Each subtribe will have its own rules, customs, and sometimes language. Some people learn the rules well enough to interact.

I was a tactical guy going into HQ with a solution to a problem well outside my identity. Consummate outsider. One notch away from turning a solution into tribal warfare.

In one move I violated four rules of monkey behavior. I had broken with my identity as the tactical guy; I was perceived to be challenging established leadership; I violated the chain of command; and I was playing outside my lane. It is telling that none of the things in my proposal were implemented until after I left the agency. It took three years to forget where the ideas came from.

Understand this: once you trigger the other person's limbic system, he or she *cannot* process your facts. Nor will that person process the facts until after the monkey issues have been resolved. No matter how right you are, no matter how unassailable your facts. Those are human concerns and the monkey trumps the human.

Had I the knowledge or the skill, all the resistance my ineptness triggered was not only avoidable but manipulable. Everything was predictable.

Had I walked into the office and said, "Captain, I know I'm just a tactical guy, but I saw that memo and I had this idea. I don't know anything about budgets, but it made sense to me, so I'd appreciate it if you'd take a look at it and see if I'm completely off base.

"I know I should have gone through the chain of command, but I figured you were the only one up here who wouldn't laugh at me if I was wrong."

I know I'm just a tactical guy. In the captain's role as protector of the future of the agency, starting by saying I know where I belong and I'm happy there doesn't trigger the status check.

I'd appreciate it if you'd take a look. Take a memo and tell one boss, "Sir, I have just solved all your problems," and that boss will shut you down. Take the exact same memo and ask a different boss, "Could you help me with this?" and he will be honored. If you want the monkey out of the way, whenever possible raise the status of the person you are dealing with.

I figured you were the only one who wouldn't laugh at me. If you are going to break a rule, have a good reason for doing so. Ideally, have a monkey reason for doing so. "The regular process is too slow" may be a really good reason, and it may be true. It is a human reason. When you present to someone in charge of maintaining the protocols that there is something wrong with the protocols, he must prove you wrong and defend himself before he even listens. If you present a monkey reason (e.g., "I don't want to be embarrassed"), his limbic system will understand.

Tactical guy + I had this idea. Coming in as an outsider is always tough. It can be deadly if you come in as an outsider to tell the in group they are wrong. That is one of the reasons domestic violence calls are so dangerous to responding officers.

If you come in as an outsider, acknowledge the fact and be careful not to come in as an authority figure. If you are there to fix "the stupid people," "the stupid people" will band together to prove you are wrong.

Whenever possible, come in as an outsider, reluctantly, to add an extra set of eyes and no agenda. The domestic violence version: "We got a call. Probably nothing to it, but it's a job, you know? Let me look around and see if I can help."

The first four monkey problems listed above relate directly to the roles of the limbic system—status, enforcing mores, and membership. The next two are subtly different.

5. **Snowflakes.** In every large organization there are a handful of people who have specific power and authority without much status. An office assistant who is the only one with access to critical records, for instance. If they feel unappreciated, they often want special treatment in order to do their basic job.

In our organization, the record clerks were "office assistant second class." That's the bottom of the barrel. I don't think we had an OA3. But absolutely nothing got done without records.

And some of the records clerks wanted special treatment. Wanted to be recognized for their value, not their official status. Any problem with that? Only if *your* monkey brain gets involved.

The people who had trouble with snowflakes were the people who wanted their own status acknowledged, who liked bossing people around. Does it cost you anything to be nice? Especially to people who have a tough, important job and get no credit?

Want to have a smooth career? Get to know the people other people don't notice. Be friendly. Appreciate them. They keep things running. Give them the credit they deserve for that.

Americans in Iraq had a magical ability. We could talk to people. One of my first translators tried to prevent me from talking to line officers: "No. He is too far beneath you. You will lose your . . ." he struggled for the word, ". . . face."

Thing was, a warden could talk to his deputy wardens, who could talk to the level below, who could talk to the sergeants, who could talk to the officers. But the warden would not talk to (and pretended not to know the names of) the officers. Or the sergeants.

The idea of talking to all levels, listening to all levels, and working as a team was an alien and unwelcome concept. But it worked. It was a superpower. And the wardens were often amazed that their American advisors who spoke little or no Arabic had better knowledge of what was going on in their own prisons than the wardens did.

---

6. **The untouchables.** There are certain groups that are largely exempt from interaction. The most potent are employees who have successfully sued an agency in the past and have let it be known that anything they dislike, anything at all, will be met with another lawsuit claiming retaliation.

Other examples are employees blatantly abusing FMLA (the Family and Medical Leave Act) and ADA (the Americans with

Disabilities Act). Those laws were written so protectively that it is legally tantamount to harassment to investigate even obvious abuse.

A third example includes legally protected classes, such as age, sex, race, religion, and national origin. An untouchable personality will reverse the intent of legislation designed to protect and use it as a weapon.

The fourth example is people who actively work at being unpleasant in order to be left alone.

It's hard to even write about this. Merely naming the groups can expose one to charges ranging from insensitivity to political conservatism to race/gender/orientation/creed/what-have-you-baiting.

That's part of the problem, of course. If you can be scared out of talking about the problem, no one can do anything about the problem. And most people do deal with this from their monkey brains, where talking critically identifies you as an enemy. As you will, but for the next few paragraphs, work to stay in your human brain with me.

Untouchables don't start as untouchables.

The monkey brain likes power. The ability to make others do things translates as safety and security. There are powers written into the laws that make some of the classes of untouchables. Most people who could use that power don't abuse it.

Taking time off to have a baby and bond with it or to care for your sick parent was the original and noble purpose of FMLA. The fact that the law was written in such a way that you could take two paid days off from work to run to the coast for a four-day weekend and as long as you called your sick mom, your employer can do nothing (and can be sanctioned for checking to see that you called) is power that some will use for their own gain.

Those who abuse the power become untouchables, but not by themselves. It takes extra work to discipline a protected class—extra documentation, more attention to detail. That creates a catch-22 because the extra work required can be taken as evidence of an agenda.

When the agency becomes afraid of this catch-22 and decides to avoid the problem altogether by not enforcing the rules on certain groups or individuals, some member of those groups will run with the power. That is natural. But the indecisiveness of the agency, the fear of confrontation, is what makes it possible.

> *I was once assigned, as a rookie sergeant, to supervise one of our legendary untouchables. A guy who did everything in his power to stonewall, dominate, or sabotage his supervisors. A man who seemed to work hard to have no friends on the job.*
>
> *I walked into his module and he immediately stood, turning bright red, staring at me and puffing up. He advanced, but before he could say a word I said, "Walk with me" and turned. He followed, and when we were out of inmate hearing, I said, "[Name redacted], I hear you're an asshole." He started to draw a breath to argue and complain, but I just kept talking: "I assume it's because you hate people and I totally get that, so here's the deal. Everything I've been able to see for myself, all the documentation says you do a damn good job, and that's all I want. So the deal is, keep doing a good job and I'll leave you completely alone. I'm required to check your books once a night. I do it twice a night, but I won't even say hi to you unless you say hi to me first.*
>
> *"Further, I'll do everything in my power to make sure everyone else leaves you alone too. If you need anything from me, you know how to get hold of me, but you're on your own. That sound cool to you?"*
>
> *It was more than cool.*

His monkey problem was that interacting with officers and supervisors was stressful. He saw the monkey games all around him and doubted his ability to compete. What better way to avoid losing a game than to make others not want to play?

And, one bad side effect—after this conversation he decided I was the only one he could talk to, so he wound up calling constantly.

2.8.2   Specific Solutions

Status Checking

In order to bypass the butt-sniffing problem, you first need to recognize, in advance, when what you are about to do will take you out of your established place. Then prepare for it. You can call it "throwing the monkey a banana so you can talk to the human." I call it "tactical ass-kissing."[2]

"Ms. Stoakley, you probably don't know me. I'm Bob Hanes, one of the engineers on night shift. I had this idea the other day and it's not really my area of expertise, but if I'm right it could save the company a ton of money. Could you take a look at it and see if I'm on the right track?"

It establishes not only who you are and where you are in the hierarchy, but that you know where you fit. You will not need to be educated by being ignored, dismissed, or patronized. It asks for help, which always flatters egos, but also shows you acknowledge the person's rank.

Will the boss take credit for the idea? Probably, but if you are working from the human goal of solving problems, so what?

Note well: sometimes furthering your career can be the human problem you are trying to solve. Something to think about.

Dominance

Whenever possible, raise the other person's status. Don't be insincere, don't flatter, but actively look for ways to make people feel good about themselves, to feel secure in their authority.

It's blatantly manipulative. Everything in this manual is blatantly manipulative, but here's the deal: all communication is manipulation. I cannot communicate, I cannot put a thought in your head, without manipulation. I have to get you to read this book. When you read it, I must use skill to make sure the message received is the message I intended.

I want you to communicate skillfully, and one of the keys is to engage with the other person's human brain. And that means not triggering his or her monkey brain. If someone feels his or her status is being challenged or questioned, much less threatened, the limbic system will kick in. Once the limbic system has kicked in, well, how

---

[2] The concept of ass-kissing bothers us because it symbolizes the most submissive possible behavior. If your priority is the job and it gets the job done, who cares? The bothering is your monkey, cringing over status issues, and you're just reading a book.

good are you at talking to monkeys in a way that gets things done?

So study status. If you have a boss who acts out, gets aggressive, and yells, instead of labeling him as an insecure little prick (labeling, hmmm?), try to take away his insecurity. If you are about to present an idea, ask for help with it instead of offering to help.

The status that you manipulate here is not real. It is imaginary status based on what the ghost community of long-dead primates values.

After a ConCom seminar in Oakland, one of the attendees reported back. She is a very intelligent, strong-willed woman. Her boss was also intelligent and strong-willed. They had been butting heads for years, almost every interaction a battle.

After the class, she decided to play up to his status instead of challenge. She reports that as soon as she made the decision she could hear her monkey brain squealing, "No!" telling her how she would lose, would be lesser.

"Do I want to win? Or do I want to get my way?" Monkey "win" versus success.

She asked her boss for his help with her proposal, the proposal he had been fighting her on. She got the proposal approved, along with his blessing. He even told her she did great work. The first compliment in years. And even though her coworkers saw what happened and wondered what her Jedi mind trick was, the whole time she could hear her monkey brain trying to turn it into a fight.

We Don't Do That Here

The only way to avoid stepping into this monkey problem is to observe the rules. If you can find a mentor when you join a group, that can be a big help, provided the mentor is intelligent and can explain things.

When possible, take care to get a mentor from the status level you aspire to. Many burned-out complainers like to take newbies under their wing and tell them the "real truth," which winds up with you sharing the label of burned-out complainer. Only accept a mentor who is successful.

No matter how careful you are, you will break small rules and protocols. Always be observant. If someone cools to you suddenly or if people nearby become quiet, you've probably just made a mistake. When the Iraqi general's bodyguards reach for their guns, you have probably made a social faux pas.

Acknowledge it. Apologize. Ask if you said something wrong. A sincere apology and interest in doing better will get you out of a lot of these errors, provided you do not repeat them. Sincerity is key. Some people use this as a tactic to avoid responsibility and continue to take advantage of others. It will work, for a while.

You talk things out with the intent of listening and improving your behavior and communication. If behavior doesn't change after the talk, the intent was insincere—it was a ploy.

You Don't Belong Here

Some people are careful to develop friendships with members of different groups and are extended the courtesy of being allowed to "cross borders." These can become your native guides. It is even better if you become one of them.

Avoid this monkey problem by recognizing tribal lines, knowing which ones are OK to cross (HR may be very friendly and approachable while IT can't stand uneducated barbarians, or vice versa). Cultivate friendships (maybe allies, but actual friendships are better) across all the tribal lines you can.

Possibly most important, recognize when *your* subtribe is insular and actively help other people work with your group.

When you have to interact outside of your group, there are three critical traits: silence, courtesy, and humility.

Silence, because it is almost impossible to trigger a negative social reaction with your mouth shut. Seriously, when was the last time you got in trouble that your words didn't contribute to the situation?

Courtesy and respect are near universals, and courtesy in almost every culture is based on not being special. Not pretending to be more important than the people around you.

Both of these, silence and courtesy, stem from humility. People get in trouble by talking, largely because they believe they are smart, they believe they understand more than they do, and they believe what they think is important. These are rarely true. If you develop the humility to assume that you don't know everything, that other people are at least as (and probably more) intelligent and experienced than you, you will have a tendency to shut up, listen, and learn. Listening and learning are both tactically good and symbols of courtesy.

Snowflakes

Wanting to be special is a monkey desire, but it triggers a monkey reaction in you as well. *Low status demanding special treatment? Ass-kissing? I'll show him!* That's your monkey brain.

Does it cost you anything to give a compliment or say please with a little more sincerity to someone who has an important job but gets no credit for it? Especially when it makes things run more smoothly?

For that matter, if you really want to get things done in an organization, identify your snowflakes, even the ones who aren't disgruntled yet, and be nice to them. Leave coffee for the night-shift janitorial staff. Remember the receptionist's birthday (or, sometimes better, remember to ask about her kids). Ask the records guy out to beer with the guys after work. Bring donuts for security (it's a stereotype, but it is appreciated).

The key is that the snowflakes are only a problem if *you* are being an ass. It costs you exactly nothing to be nice to people. Even nicer than is strictly required.

The monkey isn't all bad, and when you are taking care of the whole tribe, that's the monkey at its best. Everything works smoother.

Untouchables

If you are in an administrative capacity dealing with an untouchable over an issue of performance, I can only give you the advice your lawyers already have: document, document, document. Your own role limits you in this.

Otherwise, deal with the person, not with the issue. Many of the people who have chosen to be untouchables (see examples above: 1. *employees who threaten to sue* and 4. *actively working to be unpleasant*) have deliberately removed themselves from the tribe because they find the monkey politics stressful or doubt their ability at it.

Approach them from your human brain to their human brains. They will try to make you angry to drive you away. Treat it as someone looking for hooks. Acknowledge the specific monkey issue but do not play. Stay focused on the human problem.

"You're here to harass me again?"

"I find harassing people takes too much time and energy. I'm here to find out what we need to do to get this project done."

Most of the people labeled as untouchables have a core of skills they are proud of. If you can keep at the human level with them, most not only become good workers but can even be slowly rehabilitated into the social life of the organization. It might be impossible to completely overcome the damage they have done to their own reputations, however.

There are a few who appear to be addicted to the ability to do damage to those around them. Angry or simply mean people who actively sabotage the lives and careers of other people. Professional business consultants will call these "toxic personalities." When asked how to handle them, one said, "Fire them. It's all you can do. Fire them as soon as possible."

Monitor yourself carefully. It is very easy, and comfortable, to label anyone you have problems with as someone who can't be handled: a sociopath or a toxic personality. Those categories do exist, but they are rare. Do not use the existence of tough categories to excuse not trying. We have all been successful on some of the tough challenges because we gave them a shot and kept trying.

Remember that labeling in this way is a form of othering, is something you do from your monkey brain. When you place the person in a category, you diminish the problem-solving possibilities of the human brain.

If you must call an untouchable on a performance issue, it is critical that you remain unemotional. As much as possible, ask questions instead of making statements. Make the questions clear and stay within the rules of your workplace (most untouchables have read the rules very carefully and many are comfortable with lying about what the rules are, counting on others' *not* reading them).

So, "This is your job!" becomes, "Doesn't this fall under your job description?" Repeat what the untouchable says: "Are you telling me you don't have to do the work you're being paid to do?"

Try to handle any contentious issue in front of witnesses (generally, avoid being alone with problematic people) and document. If you keep a daily diary of work stuff that includes who you talked to and why, projects you need to work on, things you found funny, it can avoid the catch-22 of "documentation as harassment." Just be aware that such a document would be discoverable if things went to court (meaning attorneys from either side could subpoena it), so don't put anything in your diary you wouldn't want the world to read.

If you must set boundaries, be very clear: "You are required to have this process finished and to me by 3:00 p.m. If you fail, the failure and the fact that you were given a direct order will be in my daily report."

Do not get sucked into a conversation or an explanation. The most common tactic to bypass a boundary is to ask whether everyone is being given the same order. Your monkey brain will want to engage in that conversation. Making sure everyone in a tribe knows where he or she fits is what the monkey knows and loves. Don't.

If you need to explain a specific event, explain upward, to your supervisor. Your *goals* and *strategies* need to be explained downward, to the people you lead. If they understand what you want and why, they become teammates. If they do not, they see themselves as pawns.

Attempts to grow and learn for the good of the group should be nurtured. Attempts to gather power despite the good of the group (such as fishing for ammunition to make a complaint sound legitimate) or to limit your ability to do your job should not be nurtured. The most that might be necessary is, "I am being clear because I want no misunderstandings."

If you need to explain upward, the explanation should go with facts and numbers and be based on the goals of the organization:

"Chief, I'm required to have my daily report to you by 5:00 p.m. I need the reports from my people by 3:00 p.m. to make that happen. Richardson has not gotten a report in before the deadline yet. I have asked him, explained the need, counseled, and directed him four times. The dates are in my notebook and I can get them. So I gave him a direct order and will treat it as a policy violation under insubordination if necessary."

There is nothing monkey in that. Everything is based on explicit goals that were assigned by the organization.

You may be questioned on a monkey aspect: "The complaint says when he asked you if you had given the same order to others, you refused to answer."

"Absolutely, sir. On the rare occasions when someone has to be ordered to do the basic job, I don't go around gossiping about it. I would no more tell Richardson about issues with other employees than I would tell them about issues with Richardson."

Section 2.9   Group Dynamics

Generally, there are two kinds of groups, each of which has different dynamics, languages, purposes, and social rules. Both types of groups can and do exist within single organizations. That is one of the primary sources of bad communication and mistrust between levels.

Goal-oriented (GO) groups exist to accomplish a mission. Your status with the team is based entirely on your contribution to getting the job done. Hard work, intelligence, and creativity are valued and rewarded. There is no need for office parties or company picnics. It is not a social club and when the mission is accomplished, the members drift off. This last is hard for some people to understand—in bad times, a good team can be tighter than family, and then, when the bad times are over, go on to separate lives.

The ultimate goal-oriented groups are task forces or teams of specialists brought together for a single mission. Next up are tactical teams, like SWAT or special-operations groups.

Longevity-oriented (LO) groups exist to perpetuate the group. Status is based on rank and service to the group. Hard work and intelligence may be rewarded, but they are secondary to making others comfortable. Creativity almost always threatens the status quo, and is almost always discouraged in a longevity-oriented group. Social ritual, whether hazing and initiations or policy and protocol are the lifeblood of the LO group.

A pure group type is very rare. Even an extreme GO team, unless they are assembled for a single mission, will have to deal with training, logistics, and the day-to-day issues of work between missions. Even the most bureaucratic LO team still has some kind of job to do, some mission. They will also occasionally have crises that will require at least a few mission-oriented thinkers.

These types of groups can and must exist within the same organization.

Line staff, be they cops on the beat, emergency room staff, or factory workers, have a job to do: areas patrolled, patients triaged and treated, units off the production line. Failure at the job is measured by what didn't get done. Line staff tends to be a goal-oriented group.

Being a hard worker in a goal-oriented group is a compliment and is measured in tasks finished and problems solved, not in hours put in at the office. Mission-oriented teams understand looking busy and don't respect it.

Administration needs to be longevity oriented. It is their responsibility to make sure the organization survives into the future. Sure, getting the basic job (patrols, patients, product) done is important, but other things can do much more damage. Big lawsuits, lack of funding, negative media exposure can all damage the organization quickly and brutally.

Remember that to the monkey mind any major change in identity is equivalent to death. So a media exposé that forces out top administration or a civil finding that depletes the bankroll is a huge danger. They are immediate dangers, far more obvious and scarier than the slow starvation of merely failing to get the basic job done.

The jobs that administrations must do are very much about relationships. Coordinating or making deals with other organizations and businesses, arranging a budget in a government entity or fighting for a piece of the budget in a company, handling company image.

This naturally extends to a relationship-oriented outlook within the organization as well. The policies and procedures, the meetings, the organizational charts are rituals to identify and maintain a group identity.

Most large organizations will find a profound cultural rift between management and line staff.

The two groups have wildly different ideas of what is important, different ways to communicate. Both groups think they are carrying the entire organization. Line staff know they are getting the job done, and the job is the only reason for the organization to even exist. Administrators know they are the ones keeping the big wheel turning, fending off threats the line staff isn't even aware of.

It is as big and as wasteful a divide as anything commonly covered in cultural-diversity classes.

Remember the story about the memo and the budget proposal, the one where I violated four monkey protocols in one meeting?

When admin sent the memo about the budget crisis, it was never intended as a cry for help. If anything, it was attention seeking and longevity-oriented reassurance: "It's a big problem, but we're working hard to keep change to a minimum. You're in good hands."

But the memo was sent to four hundred people who measure their worth by the ability to solve problems. You never point out your own unsolved problems unless you are asking for help. There was no other way for the line staff to interpret the memo than as a plea for help.

I took the ideas to that specific captain *as a show of respect*. I wanted an old friend and good man to get any positive benefits that came from the idea.

The captain had to take it as a sign of *disrespect*. An old colleague, presuming on a many-years-old acquaintance, comes barging into his office to tell him, the captain, that he didn't know how to do his job and a simple worker bee could save a half million?

It immediately ran into the butt-sniffing problem. In the goal-oriented world, the problem of who you are and where you belong in the hierarchy is solved by showing your ability to solve problems. My instinct was to solve this issue by talking about the solutions.

In the longevity-oriented world, status is determined by your ability to follow the protocols and rituals of that world. By bypassing the protocols, everything I did read, subconsciously, as an insult or a challenge to the captain's authority.

Another example. One of the stupidest things you can do is to send tactical guys to a budget meeting.

You get the memo: We need your budget for next month's meeting.

You immediately think, "WTF? Why do we have to waste time with a meeting? It's just a damn number." Sigh.

Okay, so you get together with the key players on your team and you hammer out a number. You know there is a budget crisis, so you get the absolute lowest number—minimum required training days, backfill, ammo expenditure, nondurable equipment replacement, budget for necessary outside training, anticipated overtime budget for actual operations based on the average of the last four years . . . That's your number.

And you take that number to the meeting, fully aware that just the time wasted in a meeting that could have been handled by e-mail would cover about 5 percent of your budget.

And they ask you what you need and you tell them and they want to discuss it. WTF?

"Why do you need so much?"

"To keep people from dying. Why are we here?"

To the tactical guys, it never occurs to them that the annual budget meeting is a team-building exercise.

Scripts are unconscious and kick in faster than your conscious thought.

This is common and causes a lot of missed opportunities and grief in the business world.

There are individuals who are goal oriented and others who are relationship oriented. Though most will be happiest in a group that matches personal preference, there is extreme value in having a mix.

Goal-oriented people tend to ignore feelings and let a lot of basic relationship maintenance slide. They don't need company picnics or set up parties to mark big transitions, like promotions and retirements. A purely goal-oriented team can feel pretty sterile. Having a few relationship-oriented members can help build relationships and keep things running smoothly during quiet times. Often a goal-oriented group runs best in crisis and can become very aggravating when things are going well.

The relationship-oriented people who run longevity-oriented groups often need a few goal-oriented people. Why? Partially to keep them on track and remind the team of the need to get the basic job done, but primarily because goal-oriented people tend to respond to crises much better. Solving the problem is usually a better strategy for dealing with disaster than maintaining relationships and protocols.

It also helps for each group to have some members that can relate to the other group. Having goal-oriented people in your management team helps facilitate communication with goal-oriented teams.

Often longevity- or goal-oriented people in a group of the other orientation do not understand and can be alienated from their own group. It does no good if you are a manager who can communicate with line staff if you have trouble understanding other managers.

A common example is an employee at a low level who is not respected by his peers. They value problem solving and hard work. The employee in question spends most of his time talking, reading manuals, and visiting with his managers.

Line staff sees someone who is not good at the job and behaviors that seem manipulative and self-serving. The term, "ass-kisser" will come up a lot.

Management sees someone who values and understands relationships, communication, and the rituals of policy.

This person is on a fast track to promotion. Line staff will see it as ass-kissing and politics. Management will see it as someone who understands and exemplifies what management needs. Both groups, in their tribal monkey brains, will take the treatment of this hypothetical employee as proof of otherness.

Think of all the times you have seen someone who was terrible at a given job promoted. From the GO point of view, this is wrong. It hurts feelings and makes them angry. Promotion, after all, is a reward, and doing a good job is what should be rewarded. By GO value systems, they not only feel their bosses were stupid enough to be manipulated (or, sometimes, "They only promote their own kind"), but they feel deliberately punished for doing a good job and being overlooked.

From the LO point of view, promotion is not a reward. It is balancing the needs of the organization. People get promoted not because they excelled at the former job but because they seem like they might fit at the next level.

And, honestly, weren't some of the people who sucked at the line job pretty useful in management? And how many of the effective hard-chargers who got promoted wound up floundering and couldn't get things done?

This is why it is better to have someone who is in and of your group who understands the other type rather than someone who is by nature of the other group helping with communication. It is a cross-cultural communication problem.

Some implications of the two groups:

• Due to the vagaries of funding, bureaucracy, and labor law, government organizations are longevity oriented, even when they have a hard core of people who do the day-to-day work. When taxpayers vote to get a problem fixed, they are asking for a goal-oriented solution, but handing the problem off to a longevity-oriented group.

• A longevity-oriented group is not benefited by accomplishing the mission and ceasing to exist. They *are* benefited by being able to show incremental progress.

• An initiation in an LO group serves the dual purposes of reminding the new member that he is *very* low status and giving him a shared experience, usually embarrassing and sometimes painful, for common ground to talk. A GO group often has a test. In emergency-response groups, the tests can be exhausting, dangerous, and difficult. In more cerebral GO teams, such as tech innovation, the tests can be demanding. The purpose is to weed out those who might fail before they jeopardize the mission. The test is not inherently embarrassing; making recruits shy rarely improves mission success. It is also expected that bonding and shared stories will arise from action, not from the test.

- The fastest way to identify a group is to see who they put in charge in an emergency. If the person with the most seniority or highest rank is in charge, you are probably dealing with a longevity-oriented group. If the leadership position is decided based on specific experience or most current training and official status is entirely disregarded, you certainly have a goal-oriented group.

The dynamic between the GO and LO levels within an organization can be extremely positive or toxic. It is a symbiosis and they need each other. Generally, the organization exists for what the line staff, GO people, do—whether that is fighting crime or producing steel. The customers come to the organization for this.

But organizations exist in a complex community of trade, public opinion, politics, reputation, and relationships. In order to thrive and survive, the organization needs specialists to work these dynamics

At their best, the two levels respect each other.

It becomes toxic when the groups become enemies, when they treat each other with contempt. The most toxic I have seen was a law enforcement agency where the line staff universally believed every member of administration had sought promotion because he or she was afraid to do the job . . . and the administration thought no one would stay on line unless the officer was too stupid to take the tests.

The British Army officer William Francis Butler once said, "The nation that will insist upon drawing a broad line of demarcation between the fighting man and the thinking man is liable to find its fighting done by fools and its thinking by cowards." The toxic version of the LO/GO dynamic exemplifies this.

2.9.1 Management and Leadership

There is a saying that if you don't know the difference between leadership and management, you're a manager. But knowing the difference is not the same as putting it in words or being able to explain the difference. Almost every book on leadership I've ever read is about management and written by a manager who thought he was a leader. The notable exception is Paul Howe's *Leadership and Training for the Fight*.

Managers are systems builders. They desire to create a system, a network of facilities and policies that remove the human element. They want to believe (and insist) that all people are equal, that all officers (or workers or deputies or soldiers) are the same and should be treated the same. They believe if they can ever make a perfect system, the system will run smoothly and efficiently, regardless of the actual humans who are doing the work.

> *And this is the first twist. The managers I know are far more likely to talk about "respect" and "diversity" than the leaders I know, but the systems they create are inhuman machines. And so they "respect diversity" while trying to reduce all people to numbers, to interchangeable cogs in this inhuman machine. All the while insisting they are only trying to be fair.*

This is an amazing attempt to minimize personal conflict—to take the monkey elements out of an organization. If you're a manager, you don't want to fire people. So much easier to just be the messenger who gives them the message that under current policy they can no longer be employed. The *policy*, not the boss, did the firing. There's still conflict, but you can pretend it's not personal. As long as you follow the policies, you have no responsibility for the outcomes. Because there are no decisions.

Another way to put it is that managers try to create a flow chart without personal decisions affecting the outcome. Remove the personal element and the product will always be perfect.

And it works. It must, since management is rampant. But there are severe weaknesses to this kind of system. The first that comes to mind is the inflexibility. Reliance on emergency protocols can be really, really good—as long as you get an emergency you predicted and have a written protocol for it. Inflexibility also hurts you when you have a time-sensitive opportunity.

The second obvious problem is that there are people who excel at manipulating systems. No matter how well designed or well intentioned, bad people do bad things with good systems.

A third problem is that sooner or later, the system becomes the purpose. Hospitals exist to stay in business rather than to treat people. Governments promote and protect the parties rather than the citizens. *How* you do something (whether you followed the procedure) becomes more important than *what* you did—and so we have retail workers fired for defending themselves and paramedics who must go into more detail in their reports about the safety equipment they wore than on how the victim was extracted from the crashed vehicle.

And, possibly the most egregious example of all—under zero-tolerance violence policies in schools, the victim of violence gets punished as well as the perpetrator. This keeps the victims from reporting the bullying, which lets the managers believe the incidents decrease. The end result manages numbers at direct cost to real people.

Do you prefer leadership to management? Really? Many people prefer leadership in the abstract, but management is pervasive for a reason. Most people would rather be managed than led. Because being led demands more. It demands personal responsibility.

"I followed the policy. It's not my fault," is adequate in a system. In the kind of place where leadership is allowed the answer is:

"Policy is no excuse. You knew this would happen."

The only protection under leadership is your personal skill, and very few people are comfortable with that. Management may create a soulless machine, but a lot of people seem comfortable there. It creates the explicit rules and hierarchy that your monkey brain loves.

Leadership is about people, not policy. It is about telling people to their faces when they have screwed up and also when they have done well. Leadership is not always superior to management. It is much easier to be a bad leader than a bad manager and it has more effect. It is also easier to be a good leader than a good manager, and that has more effect too.

And that may be part of the difference. Managerial systems are designed so the cogs are interchangeable. Including the managers. So a manager, whether good or bad, will cause little change. The situation is perfect for those who fear doing something wrong more than they value doing something well.

That is a common dichotomy. For some it is a personality trait. For others it changes by circumstance. Which is a greater drive for you—to win? Or not to lose?

Organizations change over time. When businesses or teams start, they are innovative. They take risks. They work to get things done and to get a reputation. Once they become successful, there is a transition and the focus shifts from gaining to not losing. Leaders are good at making gains, but a bad leader can be incredibly destructive. As organizations grow and gain in reputation or market share, they shift toward a management-based system. They must.

I was originally puzzled that so many I talk to think of leaders as hard-chargers with little regard for others, when leadership is a people skill. Conversely, the words coming out of every HR department I've worked with have all been about valuing the individual, and fairness—and they are responsible for creating and maintaining a deliberately inhuman system.

But looked at from the twin perspectives of trying to avoid personal responsibility and avoid personal conflict, it does make sense. Thus the people who use the word "diversity" as a mantra want everyone to look different but think the same. It limits conflict. As a team leader, I wanted the widest variety of backgrounds on my teams as possible because people who thought differently would come at problems from different angles. More conflict, but we accomplished goals.

> Leadership cannot be asserted or demanded. Too many people, when they try to take charge or assert leadership, become loud and aggressive. That isn't leadership. That is what an insecure monkey does when the monkey feels threatened. It may feel to your monkey brain that it is working—people scurry. They defer. But we all know, from the outside, this isn't leadership. We call it "losing it" for a reason.
>
> Leadership is not demanded; it is assumed. If you have to prove you are in charge, it is because you know you are not. I don't know how many times I have walked into jail dorms where the assigned officer was losing control and I simply said, "Gentlemen, have a seat," and sat myself. As long as it didn't occur to me to doubt, it never occurred to the inmates to challenge. I know that sounds mystical, but it is a simple fact. You assume authority; you do not demand it.
>
> The best leader you ever had didn't scream or yell. That person was relaxed when everyone else was panicked. That's leadership.

2.9.2   On Entering a New Group

When you first enter a group, no one cares about solving the human problem or what you can contribute to solving that problem. First, people need to know where you fit. How that is handled is different in every group.

"Dagney Taggert" writes:

> *I was assigned to my division's (male dominated) narcotics team several years ago. I was soooo excited and wanted to jump in and hit the ground running. The team was small, so I thought, OK, I need to perform because being new is not going to be an excuse to not bring something to the table.*
>
> *What I thought was an enthusiastic attitude and good ideas for contacting bad guys was perceived as arrogance, snottiness, and well, not enthusiasm. I am an easygoing person and pretty much get along with everyone, so to have this unevenness in my life was terribly annoying.*

Doubly annoying—these were all guys that I knew already and got along with before being assigned to the team.

Many, many, many months of a frustrating work environment landed me in the chair of one our department's shrinks. I told him this whole story, I told him how I was so confused, how is this possible? I go to work every day wanting to work, and each day becomes more twisted than the previous. So he told me his story.

Years ago he was part of a research group and was the only male. He got along with all the women and never had an issue. Well, after several months, a new woman entered the group. He told me he noticed she jumped right in (ground running) with her ideas and opinions, and he remembered being offended, and thinking, who does this lady think she is?

But it was clear to him that the women in the group were happy with her and welcomed her input. He realized, ahhhhh, we really do work differently.

He suggested that men work in a "hierarchy" method, but women work in "group" method. So my hardworking attitude failed me for the first time in my life. Men approach a team and know they will need to work upward to gain respect. Women approach a team and know they will need to contribute immediately to gain respect.

Fast forward to last year, I volunteered for and was chosen for my division's bike team, which was all male at the time. I thought, OK, I'll approach this differently . . . I will keep my work ethic, but I'll spend the first month in a "following" mode and kind of . . . carve my niche? I guess? . . . Does that make sense?

Fast forward to present day, this team is one of the best squads I have ever worked on, and some of the funnest, craziest work in our department. My new approach served me well, as the men on the team when I first arrived there were pretty young and brash. I worked my way up, the way they all did, and gained their respect.

As I've said, many groups have official or unofficial hazing rituals, which have the dual purpose of giving you something in common with all other members to discuss and being humiliating enough to impress on you that you are a very junior, lowly member.

There will be an official or unofficial probationary period, where you are evaluated. Ostensibly, you may be evaluated on your skills and abilities, especially in a formal probation. In reality, you are being evaluated on how well you fit.

They will be testing for the things valued by the group. If they value initiative, you will be left on your own for some big decisions. If they value camaraderie, you will be invited to social events or out for a drink . . . and then they will evaluate whether you get stupid when you are drunk. Some groups value the stupidity. Like a shared hazing ritual, it gives mutual embarrassing ammunition. Also, very few people are comfortable with people who show more discipline than themselves.

Remember, monkeys like to deal with other monkeys. People who spend too much time in their human brains can be scary and unpredictable. At the supervisory course at the police academy we were explicitly told never to hire people who were "self-actualized" on the Maslow scale: "They will do what they want to do, not what you tell them to do." I disagree, but that instructor summed up the common sentiment nicely.

If you are coming into a new group, watch and, as much as possible, don't talk. Listening is rarely misinterpreted. Figure out the hierarchy, figure out how the hierarchy is determined, and then decide where you want to be. In that order.

If moving up the hierarchy is purely time in grade, that is what you must do. If it involves making big deals or flashy progress, go for it. In many organizations, especially when the hierarchy is informal, leadership goes to those who assume it.

In order to make that work, you *must* watch and figure out the hierarchy first. If you want to be one of the leaders or one of the go-to guys or one of the counselors, you must act the way they act in that organization. *Not* the way you imagine they should act.

Being loud and bossy is not how leaders act. True leaders rarely get aggressive. When you see that, it is a sure sign the person is insecure in whatever level of leadership he or she has achieved. Loud and bossy is the body language of doing a bad job and being insecure.

Watch how the leaders, the real leaders, act in your organization. Emulate them. Not just what they do but how they listen, who they listen to, what they spend time on, where and when they eat and relax.

In an informal hierarchy you will often be treated as if you are of the level you seem, and that is how you become that level.

With a new group, things are more wide open in that the top and bottom are not yet filled. The general points above remain true, but you may want to step into the leader role, and it will almost certainly be contested.

First, as in all things, decide what you want and what you are willing to pay (in time and will and aggravation) to get it. Be decisive. Do your research. Call on allies. This is the one time when having a good strategy for tackling the human problem really pays off. There are definitely people drawn to leadership roles. Some are good at it; many are not.

In uncertain times, such as the formation of a new group, people take comfort in a plan. You have to make a good plan first, of course. Then present the plan to get buy-in from as many members of the team as possible. Don't trigger monkey brains when you do this. Asking for help with a rough plan will get more support, and trigger fewer monkey issues, than arrogantly offering a solution. Also, don't be sneaky when soliciting support. A conspiracy or pretend conspiracy *can* make for deeper tribal bonds, but if leadership is a goal, sneaking is what an *insecure* monkey would do. Endorsing the plan leads to endorsing the plan maker.

When the battle for dominance comes, stay as much as possible in your human brain. Leaders only pick leaders in an established group (and far too often leaders become nothing but managers and pick other managers—see section 2.9.1). In a new group, and any group with an informal hierarchy (as well as most groups in emergencies), the people choose the leader.

Section 2.10   The Other Maslow Levels

Most of section 2, and most of Conflict Communications, centers on difficulties arising from the belongingness and esteem levels of Maslow's hierarchy. This is appropriate, since we live in a society where most conflicts come at this level.

But it is a very dangerous trap to believe the skills you have honed for dealing with social conflict are appropriate when dealing with the other levels. I am completely serious when I say that making this mistake can get you killed. Everything you know about getting along will be actively used against you by a predator.

Communication programs, no matter how good, can only work on people who are receptive to communication. A person panicked into his lizard brain will not understand words. A predator fully in his human brain (or in the very dangerous human/lizard hybrid) is a hunter who does not acknowledge your humanity. He will use communication the way a man with a shotgun uses a duck call—purely as a tool to manipulate. There is no monkey problem to solve here. You must make his human brain choose another path.

2.10.1   Dealing with Survival Fear

This isn't about *your* survival fear. If something knocks you to the bottom level of the pyramid (you are drowning or being kicked to death), your lizard will likely take over. Problem with the lizard brain is that it doesn't believe in or remember training, much less what you might have read in a book.

This section is about using your human brain to deal with someone who is operating from the survival level. That move down to survival level might be triggered by a real or perceived threat (drowning or a fire or other sudden danger that makes people panic and stops them from thinking) or by a bad drug reaction, or by a psychotic break. It doesn't matter what the trigger is or even what the underlying problem is—even an experienced clinician can't tell in a few seconds of contact whether aberrant behavior is caused by mental illness or drugs. You aren't dealing with a diagnosis; you are dealing with behavior.

What follows won't be exhaustive. See my e-book *Talking Them Through* if you need more detail.

When a prey species is battling for life, you will see the frenzy, power, and panic of survival fighting. It is rare to see in humans.

When a human is under attack by a predatory species, instincts long locked away kick in and the human tends to flail and scream or go limp. It has been centuries since understanding and acting at this level of conflict were practiced seriously. It can be a skill, but with the passing of the gladiators and the boar hunt, much of the skill has been forgotten and we are largely left with untried instincts.

Verbal de-escalation at the survival level of violence is almost always ineffective. The threat is in an older, deeper part of the mind, completely obsessed with personal survival. The lizard brain neither thinks in words nor understands them. It cannot be reasoned with. It cannot be bargained with.

What has worked, sometimes, are the same things that work on a panicked animal. A low-pitched, quiet, soothing voice. Simple words. They don't even have to be in a language the threat understands. There are some words to an Irish folksong, "Shul, shul, shul agrah." I don't even know what they mean, but they work for me.

Someone who is good with animals tends to also work well with people who have fallen to the preverbal level.

Some of the other keys to de-escalating survival-level violence:

- Make sure you are safe. Like any cornered animal, a human feeling a survival threat is dangerous and unpredictable. Try to calm the situation down verbally, but never count on it. The idea that all situations can be resolved reasonably is itself unreasonable.

- That also means you need to determine if *you* need to resolve this situation or even be there. For the officers, medics, teachers, medical staff, and other caregivers who read this, yeah, you have a duty to act. Be safe. If you don't have a duty to act, make sure you need to be there before you put yourself in harm's way.

- Be prepared to use force. These situations rarely resolve at a distance, yelling through bullhorns or calling on the phone. If the threat responds to either of those, he or she probably isn't in this mind-set anyway. Because it happens up close, if it goes bad, it will go bad at really close range with surprising speed and power. Be ready.

- Lower, if you can, the general stimulation level. Shouting and sirens and blaring radios will just frighten the person more. Dim the lights, remove unnecessary people, and keep words and motion to a minimum. Turn off music and television (use common sense—if the guy is staring in fascination at a flickering screen and not hurting anyone, let him hypnotize himself).

- Control the rate, tone, pitch, and volume of your voice. Keep everything slow, low, and rhythmic. The hindbrain, the survival/ lizard, is also the place where rhythm resides. Even if someone can't respond to your words, he can respond to the simple rhythm.

- If you must get attention, go loud, lower, low: "**HEY**, HEY, hey."

- Use simple words but don't use baby talk (the combination of high pitch and singsong and patronizing usually backfires).

- No surprises. Tell the threat everything you are about to do. Complete the description. Then do the action. "I am going to reach out with my right hand and hold your left wrist." Do it. "I am going to put a handcuff on that wrist so we don't hurt each other." Do it.

The key to de-escalating violence coming from this level is to lower the fear. Just as you must placate the monkey in order to work with someone's human brain, if this level is triggered, you must placate the lizard.

There are two general strategies: remove the trigger or remove the adrenaline.

The trigger is the source of the fear. It can't always be done and the effects may be delayed. If there is a tiger in the room, people will get hysterical. Get the tiger out of the room and the people will calm down. Eventually.

Sometimes, though, the trigger is internal or chemical. It can take months for psych meds to get to the level that some mood disorders are controlled. It can take hours for illegal drugs to get out of a subject's system. Giving time for this to happen, if you can do so safely, will usually work.

Remember two things with this tactic:

1. You may be the trigger. If the person has a history of bad relationship with you, or the person is starting to focus on you as the source of problem, or the person is afraid of what you are (a cop, for instance, or a male), you can't fix that quickly. If you have the resources, let someone else take point in the negotiation.

2. The person will not necessarily be rational and is very unlikely to be able to make human-brain distinctions. In other words, a hostage rescue team may not look any different than hostage takers. The lizard brain may only see scary strangers with guns.

Your second tactic is to remove the adrenaline. This is done with time. If you paid attention, you'll realize the bulleted list above is a guide to communicating without increasing the adrenaline. Bottom line: Never scare or startle someone in an altered mental state. Let the adrenaline leave.

That said, I've watched a man go through a full-blown screaming match at his own reflection through almost two work shifts—at least twelve hours—with no signs of letting up.

> The condition is called excited delirium. Attorneys argue it doesn't exist, but coroners have it in their manual and emergency room staff get training on how to deal with it (which largely involves getting a dose of benzodiazepines into the threat very quickly).
>
> The temperature goes way up (liver temps of over 108 degrees have been recorded at autopsy) and the threat sweats, usually strips off clothes, and often attacks anything he sees. They growl and sometimes howl and I have seen them spit blood from chewing up their own tongues. Often they try to break glass.
>
> Sometimes they fight until their own heart fails.
>
> One of my friends, years after one of these incidents, shook his head, saying, "Rory, I looked around and there were six of us and we were big guys, and we were losing."
>
> That particular threat fought until his heart failed.
>
> Excited delirium is only one of the potential causes of survival-response fighting. Sheer panic can do it. Somewhere, at the bottom of most of these cases, you will find an element of panic.
>
> It most often happens in altered mental states because the emotionally disturbed and mentally ill may not recognize when someone is trying to help.

If you are attacked by a pack of wolves, fighting with crazy strength to the bitter end is a great strategy. It might even work. If it doesn't work, it still gives the rest of your family time to get away and might even make this pack hesitate before attacking anything that looks like you. There are good reasons for humans evolving this last-ditch survival strategy.

If you must fight someone in this state, it is not like sparring or training. Incredibly well-trained martial artists forget their skills and fight like panicked animals. That does not make them less dangerous. The danger is compounded because so few people train for this kind of threat.

Pain compliance, in general, doesn't work. I don't think this can be attributed to the EDP's (emotionally disturbed person's) not feeling pain. I think he or she feels the pain just fine. Pain compliance works on an implicit bargain: if you quit fighting, I will quit hurting you. It is a communication. The survival-level threat will probably not recognize this bargain, and thus sees no good reason to stop fighting. The EDP may not remember how to surrender.

Pain compliance generally fails. Even damage and exhaustion are unreliable. Broken bones do not stop fights. The fear and emotional reaction to bones breaking makes people stop. All with the understanding that stopping fighting will keep more bones from breaking. The lizard brain doesn't recognize this, and will interpret bones breaking as losing to a dangerous predator. The only thing to do is to fight harder.

And exhaustion. Some will fight to heart failure.

What does work? Leverage and cutting off the blood to the brain.

2.10.2   Dealing with Predators

Predators can work from either the security or self-actualized level of Maslow's hierarchy. In either case, they want something from you and have othered you to the point that they will use force to take it.

The defining difference is that those working from the security level want something tangible. At many times in history and in some places today, it may simply be food or money for food. For most of the industrialized West, the motivation is money for drugs. Understand this: an addict will do for drugs whatever you would do to keep your children from starving. Think about that.

The predator working from the self-actualized level is hurting people because he enjoys hurting people. He has no hang-ups or glitches or shame about it. It is what he enjoys. It is what he does. Some very violent, ritualistic, and sadistic killers are fully self-actualized predators . . . but so are some people who just like toying with the people around them, creating drama and invoking emotion for entertainment.

For violent predators of either type, their tactics are similar.

They must choose a victim who satisfies their needs at an acceptable level of risk. They must either find that person in a place with no witnesses or get that person to a place with no witnesses. Then they must either psychologically intimidate the person into passivity or render the victim incapable of fighting back.

Choosing a victim based on needs and risks. Crime is not random. Victims are chosen. With resource predators (RP), those working from the security level who need something tangible, they need a victim with money or something that can be turned into money. The process predator (PP) working from the self-actualized level is harder to pin down. Different types of PPs are addicted to different types of thrills. Some like beating down big men. Some want to see a woman cry. Some need to hurt someone who looks like their mother.

If you do not provide the reward they are seeking, you're off the victim list. Trouble is, there's no way to know what reward the bad people around you are seeking. And homeless people rob each other all the time, so dressing down will not take you completely off the target list.

They also need someone who is unlikely to injure them. Someone who looks, moves, and talks like he or she won't fight. The meek and timid, but also the overly socialized and polite. The monkey brain is predictable. The types of violence the monkey brain allows are communication—no one really gets hurt. The predator absolutely wants a victim in the monkey brain, predictable and safe.

So prevention at this level is to lower your perceived reward (see sidebar) and to raise your perceived risk. You raise your risk profile by being assertive, comfortable in your body, disobedient when a stranger tries to manipulate you. You raise your risk profile by having friends and being cautious and staying alert.

You cannot lower your perceived reward enough to be safe. Indigent street people rob each other a lot. Unattractive women get raped.

You can, however, artificially raise your reward value. You may be in a bar and no one is thinking about robbing anybody . . . until you start bragging about your $2,000 watch or flash a roll of cash.

Does it matter how a woman dresses? Absolutely. It's not the deciding factor, but when someone dresses for attention, she gets the attention of good people *and* bad people.

Isolating the victim. The predator must get you alone. There are only a few ways to do that.

He may find you in an isolated place. We'll talk about threat assessment in the appendix. But in empty places there are normal interaction distances. If someone approaches too close in an isolated place, be ready.

The bad guy may wait. He will have a specific victim profile (say, drunk, out-of-town businessmen or athletic women). There are predictable places where that profile will be found (the parking lot of the strip club nearest the convention center and jogging trails, respectively). Learn to recognize those areas, recognize good ambush zones in those areas, and approach the ambush zones with your guard up.

Sometimes, when the victim is targeted, the bad guy must gather intelligence to know where to wait. Be very careful when giving up information to anyone who does not need to know. Strangers do not need to know where you live, or your class schedule, or that you'll be out of town on vacation.

The bad guy can follow. Learn to use reflections and shadows to keep an eye on your back trail.

The bad guy can intimidate. He may show you a weapon and say, "Come with me." He might threaten a family member. It is imperative to stay in your human brain and do the math. If you and your family are taken hostage and you see a chance to escape but must leave your family behind, it may be the best thing to do. Your monkey brain will tell you that you are abandoning the tribe. Your human brain may know it is the only way to get help.

101

If a bad guy says he doesn't want to hurt you, that sounds reasonable, right? Generally, people don't want to hurt people. Why not just go along? That's what your monkey brain will think—if you can just keep it on a script, everything will be fine. Your human brain must notice that if he really doesn't want to hurt you, why is it so important to get you to a private place without attracting attention?

The bad guy can trick you into an isolated place. Asking children for help looking for a lost dog. Telling a child that mommy and daddy were in a terrible accident and they sent a stranger to take the kid to the hospital. Ted Bundy would have a fake cast for his arm and drop an armful of schoolbooks to lure his victim closer.

This is the hardest to recognize because the essence of a trick is to mimic normal. A date rape can mirror the normal stages of courting. Who would suspect the nice guy with the broken arm would be a serial killer?

The bad guy can lure you to an isolated place. This is almost infinitely varied. Anything from offering a cheap, unlicensed cab to telling you there is a beautiful shrine just down the alley that isn't on the tourist maps.

It's hard to pass up. I have learned an incredible amount and had some great times because I was willing to be adopted by locals. With this one, watch for isolation. If they are taking you to the best local restaurant, you should see more people as you approach, not fewer.

Psychological intimidation. The bad guy does not want you to fight. He will use positioning, surprise, a show of overwhelming force, or even hope to keep you from fighting. Yes, hope. Because as long as your brain thinks this is a script, you won't get desperate enough for the lizard brain to trigger. Hope can be a paralytic.

In order to overcome a bad guy's psychological control, you must evaluate what he wants (money, your car, or you yourself), what he needs to get what he wants (privacy, silence), and your best options to get what you want (escape). This must be a cold-blooded, human-brain calculation.

Rendering the victim incapable of fighting. In certain circumstances the bad guy will attack savagely and with as much surprise as possible. Sudden assault is a problem of physical defense. It is not something where communication skills will help.

To recap 2.10.1 and 2.10.2: De-escalation, control, and communication based on manipulating the monkey brain are only effective if the other person is working from his monkey brain. It works if and only if the conflict is based in the esteem or belongingness levels, the social levels, of Maslow's hierarchy.

If the person is working from another level, whether predatory (human brain) or in the lizard brain of panic, your social skills *will not work*.

Someone scared enough will not hear or understand your words. Raising that person's status or apologizing will have no effect because the problem is not based on status.

Raising the status or self-esteem of a predator makes him more dangerous. He has already decided his desires are more important than your autonomy or existence. He has othered you to the extent that he is willing to hurt you. Placating him merely increases the sense of other, an entitlement that allows his crimes.

The lizard must be handled at the animal level—remove the fear.

Predators must be handled with human logic. Not the monkey logic of, "Let's be reasonable about this," but the cold mathematical logic of, "You won't get what you want and what you will get will cost more than you are willing to pay."

When you deal with social violence as if it were asocial, you unnecessarily hurt people. When you deal with asocial violence as if it were social, you get hurt. That's a pretty important difference.

Primary and Secondary Gains

Humans are extremely adaptable primates. They don't like wasting resources. Even a hardened predator who doesn't care about his crimes will often brag about them to get the extra social juice. He will milk an act of asocial violence for social gains—just as a few will, after a monkey dance, take the other guy's wallet. Milking a social game for material reward.

2.10.3   Affordances

Maslow gives us a convenient way to distinguish the motivations between two types of behaviors, the social and the asocial.

Social behaviors, including conflict, will stem from the belonging-ness and esteem levels of the pyramid. The conflict will be to handle social issues and will be about communication, about sending a message.

Asocial behaviors will rise from one of the other three levels. The person working from those levels will not see you as a human. At the survival level, you may be a flotation device to a drowning person, or a person in excited delirium may see a paramedic as an attacking demon. At the security level, the person sees you as simply a resource. A bad person acting from the self-actualized level sees you simply as a toy.

The social/asocial divide makes for a qualitative difference in interaction. Assassins and skilled muggers don't fight harder for what they want than bar brawlers. They don't fight at all. They hunt. And the person who wants to prove he is better than you to get the promotion is entirely different than the manipulator who will start a rumor campaign against you to deny you the promotion.

The concept of "affordances" may be the easiest way to understand the difference between social and asocial.

How you see a thing completely controls what you can do with it. If all you see is a chair, you can *only* do "chair" things. You can sit, lounge, maybe snuggle. Read a book. If you see it as a collection of flat surfaces, it becomes a shelf and a stepladder. If you see the chair as a collection of material, it can be anything from splints to insulation to a weapon.

If you don't see a problem, you can't solve it. But how you see a problem completely controls the options you have. Each way of seeing an object or situation gives you different options, different affordances.

In the social levels of conflict, you are seeing the antagonist as a person. And you can only do "person" things. And almost all person things boil down to communication. You can talk to a person, argue with a person, love a person, fight a person. You don't butcher people, or eat them, or use them to fertilize your garden, or decorate your family room. Those are all possible, but they don't occur to you. Those are not the affordances that come with the perception of a human.

Conversely, you do slaughter a steer; you don't fight it. You trade in your car when it gets too much mileage, but not your friends.

When someone is working from the asocial levels of Maslow's hierarchy, he or she has entirely different affordances than you do. To the self-actualized, you are a pawn in a game or a toy, and those people can do things they couldn't think to do to a human. Push one down the stairs because it is funny to watch. Destroy a career just to see the reaction.

The person working from the security level sees you as a resource. The addict mugger sees you as a walking, talking ATM. The coworker vying for promotion will not see you as competition, but as an obstacle. You outperform competitors; you simply remove obstacles.

And the person frightened into survival mode is in a blind panic, not seeing your humanity at all.

How you see a problem completely changes what you can do about it.

SECTION 3 TACTICS, TOOLS, TECHNIQUES

The preceding section describes what you need to know to recognize a script and choose your response. None of the material was new to you, because you have lived this process every day of your life. By making it conscious, hopefully you can now practice and develop skill.

Seeing the trap from the inside is the hardest part, but the skill improves quickly with practice.

Section 3 introduces some specific skills, both basic and advanced, that can help you manage conflict. Unlike the fundamentals, though, this is a collection of tricks. There is no direct underlying theme. This means you will have to learn and practice each of these tricks to become proficient.

Section 3.1 Coordinating Your Own Mind

Throughout the book, we have described the lizard brain as something that rarely comes to the surface, an aspect of our own personality that we know little about. That is only partially true.

The lizard rarely takes control. Only in circumstances of extreme danger does the lizard manifest and decide what you will do. But even when it is not acting, the lizard is always watching and listening.

When you get a strange feeling, that is the lizard noticing some detail and sending a message. The lizard constantly compares what it senses with your personal history. That person walks like an old enemy; be afraid. This person reminds you of your first good friend; be trusting.

We get these feelings. Many we dismiss. Some come into conflict with the monkey brain, which is more effectively emotional. Unless the lizard is triggered to the point that it takes over, the monkey often wins.

That probably sounds obscure, but concrete examples are rampant. The lizard sends a signal—duck! Or run! And the monkey says, "That might make me look silly. Let's look around first. I don't want people thinking I'm a chicken."

You get a bad feeling about an acquaintance or a business deal or even going for a drive and dismiss it: "It's probably nothing." Sometimes you regret the decision later.

You must understand that these hunches do not just appear out of thin air, nor are they products of the imagination. One of the weaknesses of the lizard brain is a complete lack of imagination.

The articulation exercise is a simple, effective way to bring your lizard (the part of your mind that notices details like an alert animal) and the human (which, it is hoped, makes the decisions) into a tight working relationship.

Next time you get a hunch or a feeling, take the time to figure it out. When you got a feeling a car was going to cut in front of you, was it because of a little "intention swerve" toward the line and away? Something about the flow of traffic and the speed that made it look like the car was reaching for a gap? Or simply that the anonymity of tinted windows makes some people feel safer to be rude drivers?

When you feel an argument about to start in a restaurant, review the body language and pattern of sound and silence for the clue that triggered the intuition. You don't need to hear the words or even understand the language in many cases, and your lizard brain knows this.

The articulation exercise really accomplishes two things. As your human and even your monkey brains learn these intuitions are based on concrete things, they trust them more.

As the intuition learns it will be trusted, it sends more signals. Trust between consciousness and the subconscious increases.

The benefits are intense. You start making better decisions faster. You see openings, opportunities, and dangers that others miss. Your confidence in taking risks increases because you trust your lizard to warn you of hidden dangers.

This is an important drill when I teach police officers. They are often required to make split-second decisions about whether to use force and how much. They almost never have enough conscious information to be sure, but the job requires that they act anyway.

The articulation exercise not only helps the officers make better, faster decisions, but it also gives them practice at explaining why those decisions were good. As you practice explaining hunches, you develop skill at replaying events mentally and pointing out the important details.

Another secondary benefit is that practice at replaying, understanding, and explaining intuition gives you a self-taught crash course in human dynamics and body language from one of the world's experts: your own subconscious.

Section 3.2 Active Listening

Active listening is a group of skills and attitudes commonly taught to officers and counselors. It's good stuff. I'll go so far as to say that active listening is *the* key element in talking down mentally ill and emotionally disturbed persons. It's also good for keeping your wife happy and staying current with your kid's activities. It makes you a better leader, a better worker, a better husband or wife, and a better parent. There is no downside to being a good listener.

Active listening is intelligence gathering, pure and simple. It is a natural counterpart of being able to read people.

What follows in this section will be a little cop-centric. That's the world I know. So you can probably ignore some of the advice about safety. In the LEO (law enforcement officer) world, any conversation or interview could be an ambush. On the other hand, if you venture into unsafe territory, it's good advice for anybody.

The two elements of active listening are that

1. you receive the information as clearly, accurately, and completely as possible; and

2. the subject wants to keep talking.

The biggest obstacle to accurately listening is that we tend to listen to the voices in our own heads first. Especially when we are emotional or we are dealing with emotional people, the conversation tends to follow very common scripts.

A cop example:

Subject: "I wasn't doing nothing. I was just walking along and he came over talking crazy shit, saying he was going to kick my ass."

How many times has the officer heard that? The officer sighs and knows that next he is going to claim he didn't even know the man he assaulted. The other guy is going to talk about some disrespect or an issue with a woman, but it will probably really be about drugs.

The officer is jumping ahead in the script. At this point he is no longer listening to what is said, but planning his response to what he expects the subject to say.

If you have enough experience, and this is a standard situation, it won't screw you up much, though you will miss a few details. You will know what the subject was lying about because the lies are pretty consistent in this script, but you will have trouble explaining to the boss or the jury how you knew he was lying. You do not remember or even hear the exact wording if you are responding to the script instead of the words.

The second aspect of this internal dialogue is the human tendency to start preparing a response before the other person has finished speaking. We want to jump ahead to the important things *we* have to say. Avoid this. Pausing to think while you are formulating a response (or even withholding a response) not only convinces the subject you are listening, but also controls the tempo of the conversation. The slower, quieter, and lower toned the conversation, the calmer and safer the situation is getting.

Acknowledge emotional states—yours and the subject's. Agitation, fear, anger, or even an inappropriate calm in the subject are valuable clues to what may come next. When you start feeling unease, fear, anger, or complacency, that is a clue as well. Is there a clue you are picking up subconsciously about what is about to happen? Is the subject pushing your buttons deliberately, trying to manipulate you? How you feel will affect how and if you listen.

One of the things presented in active listening can feel like a trick and, if done badly, can quickly put the subject on guard. Sometimes called "feedback" or "paraphrasing" or "reflecting," it is simply double checking that you understand.

The reason it feels like a gimmick is that it is often taught as a formula: "What I am hearing you say is . . ." Who talks like that? Talk like you. "Hold on. Let's see if I'm following this. Slow down, partner. The story's getting complicated. Are you saying . . . ?"

Paraphrasing, saying what you understood in your own words, is a good check with anyone, but it is a critical skill when working with a subject who does not speak English as a first language, when you are working with a foreign language, or you are working with a translator. In these circumstances, feedback is considered both polite and good common sense.

Discuss this extensively with your translator or language assistant (LA) well in advance. If not given a heads up, some LAs will take paraphrasing as an insult to his or her skills. The simple fact is that it is almost impossible to accurately tell how good your translator is. Giving and soliciting feedback is one of the ways to both assess your LA and help a poor one get the job done.

The second aspect of active listening as intelligence gathering is to keep the subject talking. The more he or she talks, the more you learn.

People like talking about themselves, so it is not hard to get most people talking.

Your focus is on the subject. Not only are you noting his or her emotional state and body language—rate, tone, pitch, and volume of voice—and proxemics, you are letting the subject *know you are paying attention.* Your eyes are focused. Your facial muscles are relaxed. If appropriate, you mention the body language in your feedback. "Partner, you said you aren't angry but your jaw muscle is jumping and I can see the vein in your forehead, so what's going on here?"

Acknowledge without interrupting—"Uh huh." "Go on." Nod. Be careful here, because many of us have practiced this as a skill to *not* listen without insulting someone we care about. It can trigger the same nonlistening mode. Remember your goal is to gather intelligence. You have to listen and the subject has to talk.

It has to be subtle, but some studies have shown that mirroring body language helps the subject relax. He crosses his arms; you cross yours. He leans back; you do the same. It has to be subtle, especially with the emotionally disturbed or the mentally ill. If someone notices you are mirroring, he *will* take it as an insult. He will believe you are mocking him.

When responding, you will paraphrase as mentioned above, ask clarifying questions, or ask questions about new or tangentially related subjects. Or you could just answer a question yourself.

Questions should be open ended if you want the other person to talk. A closed question is one that can be answered in one word—yes, no, Tuesday. "Which pocket did you have the knife in?" is a closed question. "Why do you carry a knife?" is open ended. "After he hit you, did you hit him back?" is closed. "What happened after he hit you?" is open.

Closed questions are fine if you already know what happened and are trying to lock the subject into his statements, but they can feel antagonistic or bossy and might get the subject to clam up. If you don't know what happened, or are trying to get the wording and insight you need to either disprove or corroborate a story, open-ended questions are critical.

Clarifying questions are similar to feedback, but they are not about what you heard so much as what you *didn't* hear. "You said suddenly the gun was just in your hand?" is feedback; "I'm not real clear on this: where did the gun come from?" is clarifying.

When you are asked a question, respond honestly. Respectfully, but honestly. When an inmate asked me what I thought his chances were in court, I said, "Mr. C——, you're going to get the death penalty. It's been all over the papers and people want to see you burn."

"Damn, Miller. Everyone else lies when I ask. It's bad, isn't it?"

Yeah. The fine art of building rapport with a murderer.

Some details. Your focus is intensely on the subject. That can be a tactical issue. When possible, position yourself so you can see behind you by using reflections from car windows or the subject's glasses or something else. If possible, put yourself where no one can approach your back without a shadow coming into your field of vision first.

If those are not possible (they almost always are, but if not), break contact and check your six every so often. It is acceptable to let the subject notice you doing this. Also, always watch the subject's body language. He may well see something coming up behind you and react, even if he is not on your side.

Watch your distance. A big part of both body language and safety is proxemics: how close the subject is and how close he seems to want to be.

Try not to be distracted. It allows an opening if the subject wants to go bad, and it also diminishes the returns of active listening. Your goal is intelligence gathering, not wool gathering.

When you catch a lie, take a moment before you jump on it. When stories contradict, I've had excellent success with, "The other guy said you did X. Is there anything you might have done that might have looked like X?" In the process of trying to explain away an incriminating wrinkle in a story, the subject often gives away a lot.

You can use operant conditioning in a conversation. Operant conditioning (OC, the behavior-modification system, not pepper spray) is the simple process of rewarding good behavior and punishing bad behavior.

Humans are social primates, which means social rewards and punishments work as well or better than physical rewards or punishments. In practice, when the subject is behaving in ways you don't like—getting loud, acting out, being disrespectful, or going off on tangents—give a disapproving parent look or interrupt them. When the subject is behaving nicely, give nods of approval or the little rumbling in the throat you would give to a puppy. It doesn't take much and can have profound impact over a short conversation. It also tends to work with people who have diminished mental capacity.

Be cautious in smiling during active listening, especially as a ploy or OC reward. Most people cannot consciously do the eye movement that makes a smile look genuine. A fake smile can look fake, which will shatter your rapport, or it can even look like a primate threat display. If you are one of those people who can consciously control the muscles around the eye, you can be a god at manipulating people—if you do the eye thing *only*, it is interpreted as if you really like the person but are not smiling openly to appear professional.

Contrary to some beliefs, not everything or everyone can be handled by talking. The nature of interpersonal communication is that if it goes bad, you will be at closer range than you like. Be prepared to defend yourself at all times. Do not get complacent. Practice posture and body language that puts you in a good defensive position without appearing aggressive or afraid.

If you need to shut down the conversation, shut it down. If the subject is working himself into a rage, if outside spectators are starting to escalate things, if you have two subjects who can't let the conflict go, you must be able to shut things down and take control.

As long as it is safe and working, active listening is a fine tool. Hanging on to a good tool when it is no longer safe is bad judgment. The goal is information. Always remember that information is always information but it isn't always truth.

Active listening requires a lot of work from your human brain and, with practice, is one of the most effective ways to keep from being sucked into a script.

Last note. When you are listening, you are gathering information. When you are talking, you are giving information away. What serves your purpose?

So, given that active listening is extremely powerful, why do so few people, even trained people, use the skill?

There are two reasons. The first is ego. In my own mind, I am more important than you. What I have to say is more important than what you have to say.

The second problem is the way the material is taught, especially to LEO audiences. It is often taught by an academic with promises to help officers in their world, a world the instructor knows little or nothing about.

If you want to teach anything to an adult, you must show how it is valuable in his or her world. Active listening sounds like active passivity, but "street-level intelligence gathering" is a valuable skill.

Section 3.3 The Tactical Apology

Many people, especially people in positions of power or authority, have issues with apologizing. They fear it will make them appear weak. (This is not true; see section 2.4.) Others have a problem with apologizing, believing it will transfer responsibility to their shoulders.

The mechanics of the tactical apology are simply to say, "I'm sorry you're upset." It acknowledges the problem without assuming responsibility, and it shows empathy. It can be followed by focusing on either the human problem (the issue that you are trying to solve) or the monkey problem (feelings) with a simple, "What should we do now?"

The primate pattern is that when a chimpanzee of high status bullies another chimp, the bully will spend extra time later grooming the victim. Being mean is followed by being nice. Hurt someone; then spend a little extra time making sure he or she isn't too upset.

This pattern is common, from an incident of domestic violence that is followed by flowers and cards to a boss who yells at her secretary and then gives the secretary some extra time off.

The pattern is so ingrained that if a high-status member of a group behaves badly and doesn't follow up with some kind of gesture, both parties are often disturbed by a feeling of something left undone. The "unfinished business" feeling is one of the signs of an uncompleted script.

In some cases bosses have trained themselves not to respond to the "unfinished business" feeling and can then be a jerk, day in and day out, to everybody. These are the bosses who become legendary for their poor management skills. It results in profoundly dysfunctional organizations.

There is more here in the concept of apology than we often acknowledge. It shows some things about imagining what people think and the difference, when we are in our monkey brains, of what we feel and what we know.

"Why should *I* be the one to apologize when *he* is being the asshole?"

That. Right there. That is your monkey brain.

This program is based on a few assumptions. First and foremost, that you have a job and the job needs to get done. That real status and respect are more valuable than the imaginary status conferred by our own monkey brains. That the power plays that are endemic to personal interactions don't actually resolve the social issues.

So if you don't care about getting the job done; if you want to feel good about yourself whether you have a reason to or not; if you prefer to have people give their respect to your title instead of to you, you don't need to be here. Put the book down. Go away, and continue to be a drag on your organization and your own biggest disappointment in life.

Why should you apologize to someone being an asshole? Because being an asshole is a script. It stems from an unresolved monkey problem, and he will not be capable of working on the real problem until the script is resolved. That simple. If apologizing closes the script, you apologize. Why? Because it allows you to get to work on the real problem.

But why should I . . . ? Here's another way to look at it. Why shouldn't you? If you know apologizing will resolve the issue, why would you even hesitate?

Because you might look weak? *You know that's not true.* Everyone watching knows who has been unreasonable, and likely it is both of you. You have seen yourself, time and again, that when two people get out of line, the first to apologize is *not* considered weak. He or she is considered the clear-headed one, the mature one. Even if you truly have been above the fray, apologizing is what a senior member of a group does to bring peace.

Because it might seem you are rewarding instead of punishing bad behavior? Seem to whom? In what world is an apology, a few words, a reward?

These objections are all monkey problems, your own monkey brain fighting for status and perception that does not even exist. The monkey brain is powerful. It can make killing innocent women and children with a machete seem preferable to insults and laughter. Imaginary insults and laughter, sometimes.

If it is worth it to get the job done, it is worth it to avoid our own monkey traps.

Section 3.4 Rapport Building

In Gavin DeBecker's *The Gift of Fear*, he gives a list of the tactics a predator uses to get access to his victims. I recognize all of these, not just from dealing with criminals who use them for nefarious purposes, but because these are also many of the tactics good investigators use to develop rapport with violent criminals. Under sometimes different names, many of the things DeBecker writes are explicitly taught in hostage negotiations classes as tactics to calm people down. And even salesmen use them.

Things used by bad guys can be used by good guys. The mechanics are the same. The purpose, in a way, is even the same—to get people to do what we want. What we want makes the difference between a good guy and a bad guy.

Forced Teaming

Forced teaming is the tactical use of the word "we." In criminals, this is an attempt to co-opt authority figures ("Officer, I think we have a problem here, but together we can do something . . ."), or to get a potential victim to lower defenses. By using "we," the criminal subtly places himself within your tribe. By pretending to have a common cause, the criminal co-opts your monkey mind into letting a stranger get close.

For the same reason, good guys use the tactic to develop rapport. Judicious use of "we" can make it hard to other, and thus prevent many people from escalating to physical violence. "We" can substitute for "you," and can create a team and turn around a conversation that's otherwise likely to make both parties defensive.

When the tactic of forced teaming is used with a legitimate common cause, the monkey and human brains work together to solve problems and build trust. If "we" want something that is good for both parties, not only does the problem get solved, but a real relationship builds.

Car salesmen use "we" and the appearance of common cause to make a sale. The tactic is used because it works, but buying a car is a zero-sum game. The better a deal one side gets, the worse deal the other side gets. There isn't a legitimate common cause here.

However, running a dorm in a jail (frequently sixty-five inmates and one officer locked in the same room with no separation), there is legitimate common cause: even the most hardened criminal wants as clean, quiet, and safe an environment as possible. Teaming works well to prevent problems. Once trust was established, once the inmates believed I wanted a clean, quiet, and safe dorm more than I wanted to be bossy or get shows of submission (a great attraction to the monkey mind), they would bring me problems and actively work to keep the place safe. They actually, in many cases, started to behave like citizens who care about the neighborhood.

Loansharking

Giving a small, unsolicited gift or doing a favor plays powerfully on our primate tribal core. It is one of the more reliable signs of high status within a group. Receiving such a favor predisposes us to cut the other person some slack.

Criminals use this in many little ways, some with dual purpose. Opening a door for a lady carrying groceries not only predisposes her to not suspect ill intent, but it puts the criminal in charge of the door.

Making at least a show of taking care of little comforts before an interview or interrogation is one of the ways officers put a suspect or witness at ease. This, too, has a dual effect. It builds rapport and, in men (see section 3.8) it gives some time for the adrenaline to die down, which clarifies memory.

You will also see this in a group (usually of "alpha males") who all try to pick up the check when they go out to eat.

Being nice for no reason is a powerful tactic, but it is also just nice. Making other people's lives easier anonymously and with no thought of reciprocation has incredibly powerful effects.

Typecasting

People hate being normal even more than they hate being special. It's a weird dynamic if you think about it. For all of my life, each counterculture that tried so hard to be different from their parents all wound up looking, talking, and usually thinking just like each other. Individualism has always had a uniform.

I have heard a number of rapists say (and please forgive the racism, classism, and sexism in what follows):

"All you need to get a rich white bitch alone is tell her, 'I didn't think you were like all these other stuck-up bitches that won't go out with me just because I got some tats,' and she'll fall all over herself to get in your car."

The desire to not be seen as like the others ("stuck-up bitches") overrode common sense and set these women up to be victims. People hate being told they are like other people. They especially hate being told they are like people they dislike.

As a good guy, I've used the same tactic extensively with people on the edge of violence, and the mentally ill. For those threatening violence: "An innocent person would go along with the process, sir. If you want me to believe you're innocent, don't scream threats. That's what criminals do."

For the mentally ill: "I know you are hearing voices. If you didn't hear them, what would be the right thing to do?"

That's a subtle distinction in the manipulation. A criminal will try to get you to stop acting reasonably by comparing you with the familiar. You can improve behavior by pointing out an ideal. It's the difference between, "Why are you acting like that?" and "Why aren't you acting like that?"

The Unsolicited Promise

This is something good guys rarely use. It has a high price if you expect to interact with the same people again. That's not what criminals plan.

If someone spontaneously promises something, it tells you two things:

1. What he promised was on his mind.

2. It was on his mind so powerfully that he thought you needed reassurance, even though you weren't even thinking about it.

As an absurd example, if someone walked up to you at a party and said, "Let's go to my place and I promise I won't rape you and kill you and bury you in my crawlspace with the other six," that would be a big red flag. I hope.

More common is the simple, "I promise I won't tell anybody. I just want to know the real story."

In your experience, has anyone who promised something spontaneously, without your demanding the promise or a guarantee, kept that promise?

An unsolicited promise is a manipulation. It works because we have, at the monkey level, an assumption that any conversation is with a tribe member. And once a tribe member makes the promise and asks the question, to deny is to call that person a liar. The monkey wants to talk to keep the tribal relationships smooth.

It will be used by bad guys. It should rarely be used by good guys unless it is worth the price of shattered trust. Because, let's face it, you won't use the unsolicited promise either, unless you intend to lie.

Disregarding "No"

"No" is a complete sentence. If "no" is what you need to say, in most cases it is *all* you need to say. If someone disregards your "no," it may be a sign of disrespect. That's a monkey problem. Or it could be something more serious.

If a criminal refuses to acknowledge your attempt to verbally set boundaries, he may have othered you significantly to use extreme force. Or he may have an agenda he knows is not in your best interest and wants your objections to wither. In either case, his agenda is not yours.

Often, ignoring your "no" is a test to see if you will enforce your boundaries. If the criminal can challenge your "no" and get a conversation or explanation, he has put you in your monkey brain. From that point on the criminal is in control.

I learned disregarding "no" is a big red flag—a signal the other guy is not on your side. Later, I learned it as a tactic good guys use as well.

The crisis negotiations team instructor asked the class, "If your subject says he is going to kill a hostage in twenty minutes, what do you say?"

The class took a bunch of guesses—reason, argue, put the tac team on alert. The instructor shook his head. "You do nothing. You ignore it like he never said it. You change the subject. If you argue or reason, he's still thinking about killing people. You want his mind off that subject, not on it."

It may sound counterintuitive, but it can be a powerful tactic, especially dealing with a threat on the edge of violence who is looking for hooks.

Even more—think of all the really good salesmen and how they just ignore you when you say, politely, "No, thanks. I'm not interested."

It is not enough to just ignore. That can seem like a power play to the monkey brain and increase determination. You engage the person, but on a different subject. You do not just try to distract him *from* the issue but get him thinking *toward* something else.

When someone tries to label you, to other you, it is especially powerful:

"You're a [fill in the blank]!"

"That reminds me. My grandmother was in Memphis when . . ."

There is a lot going on in this tactic. Labeling is closely related to typecasting as a tool. "That reminds me" acknowledges that you heard, even gives him credit for the tangent you are about to take, without either setting yourself up in opposition to him or his statement. In the monkey scripts, opposition reinforces.

This does not apply only to the word "no." There is a time and place to disregard any statement that doesn't serve the goal. Have you ever interacted with someone with such focus and energy (possibly a polite way of saying someone who never shuts up) that you had trouble voicing your objections? Or noticed once an objection was voiced and ignored, especially by a group, it became harder to repeat your position?

That's the skill. Use it judiciously. There is a fine line between disregarding negativity to serve a purpose and just not listening out of pure ego.

Predators are people who have othered you sufficiently to use force outside the normal social rules. They are not working from the social levels of Maslow's pyramid. That doesn't mean they won't use the skills for social purposes.

Predators also can use that mind-set in conversation. In a very real way, the purpose of this book is to teach you the valuable tools of the predator mind-set so you can use them for good. You must be aware that predators mimic the monkey brain.

When it comes to issues of conflict and especially violence, people in their monkey brains want to deal with you in your monkey brain. The scripts are familiar territory and safe, with built-in options to limit escalation.

Predators want to deal with you in your monkey brain as well. Scripts are predictable. Your monkey brain limits you from using extreme force on another person. If a predator can keep you in your monkey brain, you are the perfect prey—predictable and safe.

Whether you are dealing with a monkey or a predator, the other person wants you in your monkey brain. The predator, especially, dreads dealing with an aware, thinking human.

Section 3.5   Boundary Setting

One of the advantages of living in society with a set of rules and mores is that the boundaries are supposed to be set for you. In a homogenous society everyone has similar ideas of right and wrong, appropriate and inappropriate. The rules say who you can and can't touch and how, what you can and can't say and to whom.

These standards and many, many others are set by society. We learn them from our parents and peer group. We expect these standards of behavior to be followed, and we never really think about them until they are violated.

When standards are violated, we need to set boundaries. Because we expect society to set our boundaries for us, most of us have very little practice in setting our own. We hesitate to do so, and try to overexplain or de-emphasize the limits we set. We do this because of our fear that if we have to set rules, it might be because we are the ones who are different or wrong.

Get over that.

There are four general situations where you will have to set your own boundaries:

1. You are dealing with someone from another culture or subculture who learned a different set of rules.

2. You are dealing with someone with a different mental state or capacity who has trouble remembering, seeing, or following the rules.

3. You are dealing with someone who is on a different script than you are.

4. You are dealing with a predator who is intentionally abusing societal norms.

Dealing with different cultures and subcultures, it is usually best to be explicit, and it is OK to explain why. When people find themselves in, or travel to, a place where the rules are different, most are excited to learn the rules. That's part of the fun. It is also critical safety information.

The stereotype of the ugly tourist is the one who wants other cultures to act and believe the way people act back home. It delights in telling natives how "wrong" they are.

Like most things, it works both ways. If you are the outsider and suspect you have crossed a line, ask. Be willing to apologize and eager to learn. You can make a lot of friends that way.

Various mental illnesses and many types of diminished capacity problems (alcohol, developmental delay) make it hard for some people to understand acceptable and unacceptable behavior. Most of us learned these rules in our families, subconsciously, through repeated exposure. Humans, generally, have an instinct for social interaction and reading emotion.

In some, that instinct is missing. I have found that many people, particularly those with autism spectrum disorders, are grateful for specific explanations they can use: "John, most people only shake hands very briefly. If you keep shaking for longer than a second, they get a creepy feeling. When you shake hands, make eye contact, think 'and one,' and then let go."

Again, in many cases it is not just acceptable but a service to explain to someone with a mental illness that you are setting a boundary and why. The general rules for setting boundaries with altered states of consciousness are to

- be explicit.
- use simple words and syntax.
- keep the rate, tone, pitch, and volume (RTPV) of your voice low.
- use positive (do) speech. For example, say, "Talk quietly" instead of "Don't be loud." Tell them what to do instead of what *not* to do.
- work from the common ground. If dealing with someone delusional, neither challenge ("You're not really seeing that! Get real!") nor accept ("Hey, I see the blue men too.") the delusion. Concentrate on what you both can see.

Certain mental illnesses will have boundary issues, not because of an inability to understand the social rules, but because of an inability to maintain self-control. Boundary setting in this situation must be clear and explicit. And probably loud: "Back off!" or "Get out of here!"

Like boundary setting with a predator[3], you must be able and willing to enforce any boundary you set.

When someone is dealing with you from a different script, or a different place on the same script, you will have to set clear boundaries.

Acquaintance rape is an example of a script disparity problem. It is a variation on a standard mating dynamic: mutual attraction, talk that includes availability signals, *find place and time to be alone* and explore each other as a couple.

---

[3]It would be convenient if an individual could be either mentally ill or a criminal but not both. The reality is that not only can people be both, but that many criminals will claim mental illness in order to have an extra set of excuses to act out.

The space and time to be alone is what a predator looks for. It is also what young couples look for. Predators are good at reading this dynamic and exploiting it. However, stupidity, immaturity, and self-centeredness can bring this script to the exact same ending as willful evil intent.

As the mating dynamic progresses and more time is spent alone, the couple increases their feelings of security. They then increase the physical intimacy. Both people have an internal, usually socially set, boundary for how fast the physical intimacy should escalate.

If the boundaries are similar, the relationship could be strong. If the woman goes faster than the man, you often get the, "She's fun, but not the type you take home to Mom" reaction. Young men almost never set boundaries to try to get the woman to slow down.

If the man goes faster than the woman, which is common, the woman will have to set boundaries—a clear "NO!" And back it up.

In most cases, the man respects the boundaries and slows down. How he handles that will determine whether the relationship continues. Women gauge and set a value on how a man responds to requests and boundaries.

If the man does not respect the boundary, it can escalate to rape.

Boundaries must be enforced. If they are not enforced, the threat quickly sees them as not being boundaries at all. That said, enforcement does not always mean fighting . . . and fighting and struggling are very different things.

If a man escalates intimacy beyond your comfort level, the first boundary is a clear "no." If that is ignored, enforce the boundary by *leaving*.

A woman has every right to defend herself by physical force. That is an absolute fact. However, the first priority is to get you out intact, not to champion your rights. Leaving is the better first option.

Here's the reason: guys in a hormone cloud can be pretty damn stupid. Add alcohol to the mix and it's worse. And there are some terrible cultural norms—it was never true love until after Maureen O'Hara slapped John Wayne. If you slap him or push him or pound on his chest, even if you hit him with a closed fist in the jaw, a man who wants to badly enough can choose to misinterpret the signal. Combined with the fact that the woman is still there, he may even read the strike as an increase in physical intensity.

Leaving is harder to misinterpret. It makes it clearer that he has crossed a line. If he tries to stop you from leaving, that is the signal that this is a predatory act and must be treated as a predatory act. Use force and do it right. Muster all of your cunning, surprise, power, and tools to put him down and make yourself safe.

Understand that saying there is a difference between predatory date rape and date rape devolving from a toxic script does not imply that one is bad and the other good, or that one type of rape is wrong and the other is "just" a mistake. Both are wrong. Both are evil. It's like tigers and sharks: both can eat you, but the tactics for avoiding them are different.

Most alternate-script problems are not as high stakes as the acquaintance rape. Salesmen learn to keep you on the script that ends with you buying. They ignore your attempts to change the rules.

Dealing with a predator who intentionally abuses the social norms, the boundaries must be clear and forceful. You must be ready to back them up.

A predator wants something from you. He is not willing to do absolutely "anything it takes" to get it. He doesn't want to die and doesn't like pain. Predators make very cold-blooded risk/reward calculations on their actions. So you set the boundaries and make sure the price will be higher than the predator is willing to pay.

Do not negotiate, talk, or explain. "No" is a complete sentence. The predator wants to deal with you in your monkey brain, and he will play on your social insecurities. "Why do you have to be so mean?" "Don't be like that, honey" "Why would you even think that?"

If he can get you into a conversation, your boundaries become negotiations. They aren't boundaries at all. If he is a violent predator, he will use the conversation to get close enough to attack.

Remember not all predators are violent—users and manipulators use exactly the same tactics.

Section 3.6 Work from the Common Ground

This is one of the most important basic ideas. When dealing with a rival, an enemy, an emotionally disturbed person, or across a cultural barrier, *don't* dwell on the differences.

Everyone is different, but we are all similar enough to communicate. Communication works from similarities.

When a schizophrenic says he is hearing voices, he is hearing them. Simple fact. To deny it, to say, "C'mon, you know that's all in your head" is not only insulting, but it denies the fact that hearing voices is not a choice. To agree is even more insulting. "I think I hear them too" is a patronizing lie, and most schizophrenics will pick up on that right away.

"You know I can't hear the voices. I can hear the kids in the park and traffic." Concentrate on what you both hear, what you both see.

Why is talking about the weather such a cliché? Because it is something we all share. We all experience the weather and it affects every one of us.

Cross-culturally, talking about politics and religion is problematic, or can be. Talking about food and family and the countryside is usually good common ground. There are exceptions. In Arab culture, it is expected to ask about a man's children but it raises suspicion if you ask specifically about his wife or wives.

Even talking about the problematic areas, like religion, the common ground is still generally safe and helps to build bridges. What is the common ground of religion? It is all the questions that religion exists to answer.

If I tell you my answer and you tell me yours, we have an argument. If I tell you my question and listen respectfully to your answer, we have a friendship.

Sidenote: Rarely initiate conversations about politics or religion. That can sound critical or like you are throwing out hooks. It is hard to tell how involved someone is with surface interaction. If you get a hint that the person is deeply interested, though, ask questions. It is almost impossible to ask a sincere question disrespectfully.

People like talking and they love teaching. Listen. Use the active listening skills and talk as little as possible.

> I was trying to explain to a high-ranking officer that he needed to train his lieutenants in both leadership and management.
>
> My translator froze. "Mr. Rory, in our language those are the same words."

Never assume infinite common ground. Your values and beliefs stem from your culture, and things that are clearly right or wrong in one place may be merely interesting or inconvenient in another. When you discover a breakdown in communication, backtrack a bit, find the common ground, and build the understanding piece by piece.

> It took a half hour to make sure we all understood, but we boiled it down to, "Telling people what to do by sending them memos is management. Being the kind of person who makes troops want to be like you and make you proud, that's leadership."

In hostage survival training, we were taught to "personalize" ourselves. The theory is if the hostage takers know you as a person, know your name and that you have children, it would be harder for them to kill you. That's mostly true. If the hostages were Zero Population Growth terrorists (I don't think such a thing exists; this is an illustration), telling them you have six kids would *not* make it harder to kill you.

Here is the underlying mechanism. In order to use significant force, to kill you, the killer must other you. Hostage situations sometimes last long enough that a relationship develops. Your job is to guide that relationship, to find the common ground.

All of us are members of many different tribes—our state and nation, our belief systems, our schools, our hobbies, our jobs . . . even sports teams.

> *"I fucking hate cops."*
>
> *"Partner, this is just a job to take care of my family. What I really like is going fishing with some friends and havin' a beer."*
>
> *Especially if you saw a wedding ring on his finger, smelled alcohol on his breath, and saw a fishing pole in the back of his truck.*
>
> *He has tried to place you in the enemy tribe of "cop," but you have placed yourself in three common tribes—family men, drinkers, and fishermen.*

Section 3.7   The Power of Reputation

A book like this will give you tools and understanding, but it will not change who you are. The people around you already know who you are. Maybe not, in some cases. Serial killers sometimes hide in plain sight for extended periods. Office manipulators occasionally work below the radar for years. The janitor next door might give thousands of dollars to charity every year and never tell anyone.

But the people around you already know if you are reliable or not. Trustworthy or not. Whether you care about them or only about yourself.

The script is not in the words. It lies in the patterns. You can sometimes follow a script in a language you don't know.

> *One of my favorite supervisors of all times was a vulgar slob. He regularly used language that would have gotten anyone else sued. He never got a complaint.*
>
> *It took a while, but I realized that despite the words he used, he was always there to help. Anyone, anytime. He used terribly offensive language, but he was scrupulously and naturally fair in his behavior.*
>
> *If you needed help, he was there. If you needed someone to talk to, he was the one you turned to. When he said, "Fuck you, fuck you very much," in the Elvis Presley voice, you just smiled and shook your head.*
>
> *The worst supervisor I ever saw was scrupulously correct. You would never find a hair out of place or hear a vaguely inappropriate comment. But this supervisor seemed to hate the troops and actively worked to sabotage careers and the job. This one took delight in finding and punishing the slightest wrongdoing.*
>
> *When this supervisor said, "Good morning" and smiled, you started looking for the knife in your back.*

You do not get to pick your reputation. You can decide until your head explodes that you are a good person who takes care of others. You can say it a million times—but only taking care of others makes it true.

Everything in this book is a tool. It can show you ways to understand how communications go wrong and how conflicts arise. It might even give you the understanding you need to make some profound changes.

Just reading it will not change you from a bad person to a good person.

Perhaps this is more a caution than a tool: your reputation is based on the way you treat people. It is never based on your reasons or excuses. If your reputation is cultivated over time, it will grow into one of the more useful tools in your repertoire.

A good reputation will give you some protection from honest mistakes. A bad reputation will undermine everything you do.

Section 3.8 The Human Alpha

The term "alpha male" gets a lot of play. In my experience, usually authors with little or no experience in biology take poorly understood wolf studies, combine them with poorly understood chimp or baboon studies, and then try to extrapolate to people.

It doesn't work very well. Humans have more privacy and wider mate-selection rules than either of the other species. We do not live in as small of bands, nor do we have to hunt as tight teams to survive like wolves.

So what is a human alpha? It is someone who shows up with more resources to solve other people's problems.

Being a leader does not make you an alpha. If you create problems, you are a bad leader, not an alpha.

Being bossy and loud does not make you an alpha or a leader. Being bossy and loud and getting problems solved *can* make you an alpha, unless you create more personal problems than you solve.

Being a manager, even a good manager, doesn't make you an alpha, not unless you show up. Leadership and helping has to be personal to earn the status.

If you show up to help people, even just with more psychological resources so they have a shoulder to cry on, you are an alpha. An alpha isn't always a leader, but a human alpha is always respected.

The formula for respect is simple. You have more resources than the people around you. It may be money or power (what most people think of when the word "resources" comes up). But often it is insight or knowledge or compassion or a simple willingness to work.

If you do not have more resources than those around you, you are dependent. You are a child. There is no respect in that.

If you do have more resources than those around you and you use those resources only for your own purposes, you are a selfish jerk. There is no respect in that.

If you do have more resources than the people around you, and you use those resources for the good of others, you become an alpha. There is immense respect in that.

Resources + Helping Others = Respect

Note well, though. You must help people with their problems, not what you choose to believe their problems to be. That's the way of at best a busybody and at worst a tyrant. There appears to be no limit to the evil a group can do if they can convince themselves it is for the greater good.

Section 3.9   Manipulating Adrenaline

Adrenaline is a trigger (or maybe a side effect) of the various emotional states. That means there is almost always an element of stress hormone production when conflict is expected, whether it is the fear of imminent death that triggers the lizard or an imaginary fear of loss of status that triggers the monkey.

Different people have different reactions to adrenaline, and there is a notable gender difference.

Generally, men have a big spike of adrenaline that lasts a short time and fades quickly; women have a long, slow buildup that lasts a long time and tapers off slowly.

When I get in an argument with my wife, she is calm and reasonable—which I take as a sign that she doesn't understand. I get angrier; she stays calm. Then I go for a walk to cool off. A few minutes later, I'm calmer and I realize she was right and decide to go back and apologize. I walk home, open the door, and start to say, "Honey, I'm sorry . . ." and she lets me have it.

Early in the argument, she wasn't being calm and reasonable because she didn't get it. She was being calm and reasonable because her adrenaline hadn't triggered. This means she was thinking clearly, which is a solid indicator that she is probably right—but I am stuck in my limbic system and can't see that.

When I have cooled down and return to apologize, she is just hitting her adrenaline . . . and she can stay mad a lot longer than I can.

I've used this difference to plan cell extractions. In a cell extraction, the job is to go into an enclosed place with an extremely violent criminal and (ideally without injuring that criminal) remove him or her from the cell. It means you have to go through a door on someone who is completely ready, willing to do violence, and possibly armed.

When the inmate was a male, to manipulate his adrenaline, I would go through the routine sequence of ask/advise/order/check.

Ask: "Sir, please turn around and let me handcuff you."

Advise: "Sir, if you do not let me handcuff you, I will have to use force up to and including . . ."

Order: "Sir! Turn around now!"

Check: "So, you are telling me I have no choice but to use force. Thank you. That makes the paperwork very clear."

Then I would add the manipulation: "You know what? I'm tired of talking. I'm going to get six guys and some pepper spray, come back here, hose you down, beat you down, and drag you out by the hair. I'll be back in ten minutes."

The subject would have a huge adrenaline spike that would be waning in ten minutes. But I'd come back in twelve and say, "Crap. I forgot all about you. I'll go get those guys and come back and kick your ass."

Another adrenaline spike, but not as high. When I came back this time, the subject almost always complied without force.

I would never dare use that tactic on a woman. Unlike men, women can plan what to do before the adrenaline hits. Had I threatened to come back in ten minutes, a woman would have used the ten minutes to make armor, weapons, and soap the floor. And would have been in her full flow of adrenaline when it was time to fight.

Chris McKaskell of London, Ontario, has used a variant of this tactic on one of his employees with a temper. "When I want to talk to him about something that might set him off, I make him angry about something else first, like his football team sucks. Then I come back about ten minutes later with the real issue."

Section 3.10   Brown M&M's and the Purple Rose

Van Halen (ask your parents) had a clause in their contract that said when they got backstage before performing a concert, there was to be a bowl full of M&M's with all of the brown M&M's removed.

Egotistical assholery or brilliant stratagem?

Stratagem. At the time, Van Halen had one of the most complicated road shows in rock music. The contract was long, complicated, and included exactly what they needed for power outlets, construction . . . all that stuff. They had included the M&M clause because compliance was easy to see. If they arrived at the venue and saw those instructions hadn't been followed, they could be sure the rest of the contract hadn't been read and therefore knew they needed to get an electrical engineer to the venue to save the show.

I've frequently vetted new acquaintances with a variation—tell a juicy story in confidence and see if and when it comes back to you.

One of the snowflakes (she is a "mere secretary" but absolutely runs a major city's training department) deliberately puts a typo in every contract. If you don't bring it to her attention, she classifies you as unprofessional and you will not receive a contract from that city again. Smart.

The purple-rose tactic comes from a web designer who puts a random flower on every site she creates. She has found that her client points out the flower, she apologizes, and the client doesn't ask for any more changes.

Some people, especially some supervisors, are driven to mark their territory and assert their status. They need to order their underlings to change something or they feel they are not being supervisors. So you give them something to change. Assuage their monkey brains.

One of the most egregious examples was a lieutenant who returned all reports for rewriting. I figured it out early when I waited twenty-four hours and then turned in the exact same report. She looked it over and said, "That's a hundred percent better. Thank you."

One of my friends took a different tack. His wife was an English teacher and he sweated until he handed in the perfect report—no typos, no grammar, spelling, or punctuation errors, perfectly formatted to policy. And the lieutenant ordered him to change a fact. Rather than falsify a report, he made a deliberate error in every report after that.

Two things:

1. It is very hard to recognize yourself, but if you are this kind of supervisor, stop. This is pure monkey brain, completely unnecessary, and what you are seeing as strict supervision your people are seeing as contemptuous insecurity. Generally, you don't have to make people do good work. Just let them do good work.

2. If you are that supervisor and you now start looking for two mistakes . . . sigh.

Section 3.11 The Grand Recalibration

You now have the bones of the program—the background, the principles, and a collection of tricks. You can never go back. Even if you reject everything in the program, even if you refuse to admit how often your monkey brain has controlled your life, it will never again be invisible to you.

That is going to change your life in two profound ways.

Number one, the monkey hates losing. It fears a loss of status. And now that you see you are being manipulated, that other people are using—more, *relying*—on your monkey brain in order to control you, the monkey brain is going to start doing something odd. It is going to start ordering the human brain to think of a way to win. To not be manipulated. For completely monkey reasons, your monkey is going to order you to spend more time in your human brain. And I'm OK with that.

The second—as successes pile up, as your monkey brain starts seeing how well this works, as it sees your real status with real humans rise as opposed to imaginary status with imaginary chimps, your monkey brain will change its definition of the best monkey.

All of your life, no matter how stupid it was, you have been wired to do the things chimps admire. To be the strongest, the biggest, the most stubborn, the loudest.

Now your monkey brain will start changing that definition to being the smartest and cleverest monkey.

As the fortune cookie says, "Your life is about to change."

APPENDIX I VIOLENCE

Violence: (1) Swift and intense force: *the violence of a storm*. (2) Rough or injurious physical force, action, treatment: *to die by violence*. (3) An unjust or unwarranted exertion of force or power, as against rights, laws, etc.: *To take over a government by violence*. (4) A violent act or proceeding. (5) Rough or immoderate vehemence as of feeling or language: *the violence of his hatred*. (6) Injury, as in distortion of meaning or fact: *to do violence to a translation*. —from dictionary.com

Levels of Coercion

Violence has a pretty broad definition. It's important to understand it from various levels and points of view. To my closest friends, violence is "that level of human interaction that requires a lot of paperwork." That sounds flippant, but it is one point of view.

Other people consider an argument or verbal intimidation to be violence.

It is easier to see in terms of coercion. Coercion is forcing someone to do what you want. It always has a level of violence to it, though that violence may be only verbal or psychological. It may not seem like violence to you or to anyone else watching. For our purposes, these levels of coercion can be seen as levels of violence.

At the lowest level are *nice people*. Nice people get along. They care about each other. They have a job to do and they care about the job and they get it done. Nice people are easy to get along with. They create an easy, comfortable environment to live and work in. Is there coercion here? Yes, but it is subtle and light: if you don't act like a nice person, the nice people will chill you out. Ignore you. Not say "hi" in the morning or invite you out after work.

Some people see this as a horrendous thing, a drive to conformity, and a form of horrible social injustice because, evidently, they want the right to be jerks but still be treated as if they were nice people by nice people. Whatever. Grow up.

Groups of nice people get along until they are hit with the next level of coercion: the manipulative. The *manipulative* person uses rumors and lies and backstabbing to get what he or she wants and be damned to the nice people.

The manipulative person hits the nice people like a shark in a tub of minnows.

Nice people tut-tut and say, "He's playing politics," but they don't know what to do. They don't honestly understand how some-one can be so selfish or so mean. The manipulative person easily man-ages image and frequently moves up quickly.

From the nice point of view, the manipulative person is mean. The violence is subtle, not physical, but the victims are truly victims, subjected to things they don't like. Nice people don't understand the manipulative person at all.

The manipulative person sees nothing wrong. He or she is just getting things done and feels, at most, pity for the others who "just don't get it."

"This is the way the world works," the manipulative person thinks.

The manipulative person will run roughshod over the nice people until he or she runs into an *assertive* individual. The assertive one will stand up to the manipulative person and say, "I know what you are doing. Knock it off or I will stop you." The threat is not one of violence, but of invoking policy or spreading the word. Manipulators fail when exposed.

Assertive people see nothing wrong with what they do. It is basic boundary setting. It is also something held up in our society as a goal. I applaud that—assertive people tend to be more up-front and easier to deal with—but nice people, while admiring the concept of asser-tiveness, describe assertive people as "pushy and demanding."

Nice people see the assertive ones as pushy and demanding. The manipulative people find them confrontational. Just as manipulators see nothing wrong with their level, they see the assertive level as wrong. Confrontational.

Assertive people do well and they tend to be very effective. They will go along in the job . . . until they meet an *aggressive* person.

Even an extremely assertive person tends to crumble when someone charges into the office screaming threats and frothing at the mouth. This is just outside the edge of what society can quietly ignore. The threat of physical violence is implied, just under the surface.

Some bosses make a career out of being loud, threatening bullies. It cows the nice people and the manipulative people, and keeps the assertive ones in line. The aggressive people feel like big men or women. Strong, feared. They see nothing wrong with what they do, maybe admire their own bravery. They call it "brutal honesty."

To everyone else, of course, they are asses. Way out of line. Totally unacceptable behavior. But no one who works from a lower level can deal with them or even really understand them.

The aggressive person will rule the roost . . . until someone slugs him. Aggressive people are totally unprepared for the *assaulter*. When they run into someone who is willing to deal with the carefully implied threat of violence the blustering bully relies on and act with real violence, it is a huge behavioral line. Most of the aggressive cannot cross it. An aggressive person, who was completely comfortable with his own behavior, his level of violence, is outraged by an act of physical violence. He might have been loud, maybe a little mean, but at least he never hit anybody.

The assaulter has some mental gymnastics to do. Smacking someone is socially condemned pretty universally, so most justifications are event specific: he made me mad. She should have known better. He had it coming.

In the end, though, the assaulter is comfortable with handling things physically. And, as it works more and more often, the assaulter sees more and more use for it. If he gets very comfortable with assaultive force, he can prey like a wolf on the other levels.

Until, of course, he meets someone willing to use *lethal* force.

The levels, in order:

- Nice
- Manipulative
- Assertive
- Aggressive
- Assaultive
- Lethal

There are gradations between levels. Within the assaultive level, shoving is easier than striking. At the murderous level, bombing can be abstract, but stabbing rarely can.

And there are levels below "nice." One is the "pleaser personality," who offers himself up to be manipulated and used, who thinks acceptance and even love can only come from giving in to others. More damaged than this are the groomed victims, the individuals who were taught as children that "Daddy shows he loves me with his belt" and actively seek a violent codependent relationship because it is the one tribe where they know the mores. They know how to function.

People are comfortable with the level they live at. The level above theirs is the level, no matter where it is, that they consider wrong or violent. People are completely unprepared for dealing with a higher level—they do not have tactics and generally can't understand the motivations or the people who work at a higher level.

Universally, they consider people who function at a lower level to be weak.

The level above yours is bad; the level below yours is weak.

This has some huge implications, especially for communicating between people who function at different levels.

If you have lived for some time at a relatively high level (such as many infantry soldiers, patrol officers, and corrections staff), many of the things that happen at a lower level, like office politics, seem petty. When part of your job involves occasionally being shot at, anger at someone not contributing to the coffee fund doesn't seem that important—and you wonder about the people who do get excited. (I confess to having said publicly that if you know or care who is getting married or divorced in Hollywood, you need a life.)

When we tell our spouses to stand up to the boss, we know he will back down. We deal with things at high levels of coercion and know what it will take to make a manipulator crumble. But we sometimes miss that asking a nice person to be assertive is asking that person to jump two steps beyond his or her comfort level. It is often asking someone to be what he or she perceives as "bad."

Conversely, people who are comfortable at higher levels of coercion often exhibit an attitude that frightens those who live at a lower level. As the T-shirt says, "Killing you is the last thing I want to do, but it's on the list." It is on the list for only one level of individuals, and that bothers the others immensely.

Understand, this is not about right or wrong or which side you are on. Effective soldiers and officers who have time and again proven their loyalty, self-control, discipline, and honor often find that the people they defend are afraid. And many of their bosses work from the assertive or manipulative level and find the trigger pullers very disturbing.

Going down levels is easy. You will never find a murderer who can't bring himself to lie. Though the skills are very different, you will not find a sniper who has ethical issues with hostage negotiations. But you will find negotiators who could not take a life.

Going up levels, using a level of coercion you have subconsciously categorized as "bad," takes great provocation.

> *Shortly after the formation of our CERT (Corrections Emergency Response Team) a psychologist asked to observe our training.*
>
> *The goal of CERT was to handle any situation regular staff wasn't trained or equipped to handle—cell extractions on armed inmates, riots, hostage rescues. At this stage in our development, we had no firearms and limited weapons of any sort. No Taser, some pepper spray, batons. We were expected to handle situations that would normally be assigned to SWAT, in a building that amounted to a fortress, and do it primarily hand to hand.*
>
> *As such, the team was handpicked to be extraordinarily skilled and extremely cold and controlled fighters. They were men and women who regularly and successfully fought against bigger threats or multiple opponents, but also had the reputation for never losing their cool or using excessive force.*
>
> *The psychologist wanted to watch us and I watched her. Much of the early CERT training was in team tactics, how to use our numbers to take down a threat without injury. One memorable day, the psychologist spent all morning watching us. We were beating merry hell out of each other, using force and techniques that she had trouble imagining, and we were having fun.*
>
> *Then we got the call. A cell extraction, right in the building. She watched us switch from laughing and brawling to arming up and planning. Everything went to grim silence. Andy and Shawn made the hasty plan. We loaded up in the elevators for the long ride to the jail floors.*
>
> *The psychologist hesitated, but she went along. Her eyes were wide and her knuckles were white the whole way. When we got to the floor*

where our really bad guys were housed, there were ten silent people dressed in black staring blankly at a door.

Inside the door an inmate, screaming threats, claimed he had weapons and would kill us all.

Andy walked up to the door and introduced himself. Then he said, "You know why we're here, right? I want you to turn around, put your hands through the food port and let me cuff you. Otherwise, I'm going to let these guys loose. Whatd'ya say?"

The inmate decided to be cuffed. Completely silently, the team searched the inmate and the cell, and then transported him to a higher-security area. When the team was in the elevator with no more inmates in hearing, the silence shattered, "All right!" "High five!" "Perfect operation!" "That's what I'm talkin' about!"

The psychologist's jaw dropped. After watching for a morning the level of brutality we used on our friends and how much we enjoyed it, she had been terrified of the level of force we would use on a real threat. She thought of us as thugs and expected murder.

Going down levels is easy. Professionals who are authorized and skilled at deadly force talk down thousands more than they kill. People who can't grasp high-level force fear, at a very deep level, those who can.

APPENDIX 2   THREAT ASSESSMENT

There are four basic questions that fall under the heading of threat assessment:

1. Is this a dangerous relationship?
2. Is this a dangerous place?
3. Will this situation become violent?
4. Am I being targeted for violence?

Understand that there are always outliers. Every so often, a mentally unbalanced person does take a weapon and go on a shooting or stabbing spree. Unless you have a personal relationship with the attacker, there is no way to see this coming. Very rarely, a normally peaceful person develops an extreme case of adult-onset schizophrenia and explodes into violence. There will, until we as a species know much more, always be a small number of random acts of violence. But in most cases violence is part of a pattern.

Is This a Dangerous Relationship?

This is the easy one because you already know the answer. If there has been violence in the past, you can expect violence in the future. Your monkey brain will want to deny this to keep the relationship going, and the violent person will also want to deny it, to keep the relationship (and access to a victim) going. You cannot afford to deny it.

Will it escalate? Not always. Some domestic violence cycles have continued for a lifetime. If it is escalating, the human-brain choice is to leave. If it is not escalating, the human-brain choice is still to leave, but no one can make that choice for you.

If and when you decide to leave, I suggest reading one of the chapters from *Campfire Tales from Hell*, "Checklist for Leaving an Abusive Relationship." In a book of essays, largely written by tough guys, a woman writing under the alias "Jael" penned something that isn't an essay or a story. It is just what it says, a checklist. A checklist for leaving an abusive relationship. It may be the most chilling and important chapter in the book. It is good advice from someone who has been there.

That said, there are some signs to watch for in a new relationship.

A series of prior bad relationships is a red flag. Especially if those relationships were violent. It is very unlikely that you will find this out from the person you are getting to know. Violent people rarely have a problem lying. But if you find out from other sources, it is unlikely the next relationship will be peaceful.

Looked at in ConCom terms, everyone has a tribal idea of what a "normal" or "good" relationship should be. A history of violent relationships indicates this person knows how to function and may only know how to function in a violent relationship. Resetting an adult's idea of normal is very difficult, if not impossible.

One of the clues—**if the person describes all of his previous partners in negative terms**—you will hear, "My first ex-wife was crazy and my second was worse." You probably won't hear, "I couldn't control my temper." What are the odds that all of his previous partners were crazy or mean? He is the common denominator in all of those relationships.

If the person has no old friends, even if he or she seems quite popular.

If the relationship is accelerated, charming predators are masters of the whirlwind courtship. They know they can't keep up the gallant façade for very long. They also know the further the relationship has gone, the more invested you will become in it and the harder it will be for you to leave.

> *Years ago a new nurse—kind, loving, and compassionate—asked my advice. She wanted to take an inmate home and wondered if she would get in trouble. Duh, yeah. Fired. She explained that the inmate was a "really sweet girl" who had never been in trouble before and had no family and no place to stay. She got all this right from the inmate who had "no reason to lie" and had no idea the nurse was thinking about offering her a place to stay.*
>
> *When dealing with criminals, always check facts.*
>
> *I took the nurse over to the computer and ran the "really sweet" girl's extensive criminal history over the previous ten years. Drugs, theft, prostitution, domestic violence . . . she'd lied about every last detail and nearly gotten a nice person to throw away her career on a good deed just so she could have access to a home, a place to shoot drugs, and money through theft, intimidation, or (once the nurse realized she could be fired) blackmail. Gamed.*

When the rapport-building techniques from section 3.4 are used to get you to do things you don't want to do. "Try some meth. What are you, chicken?" is typecasting. When someone ignores your boundaries, he is discounting "no." Rapport building can be done ethically and respectfully. When it is done to disempower you and empower the other, you are being set up.

Separation from resources. Speaking of disempowering, if someone tries to cut you off from your friends, or limit access to your own funds, or control where you go and who you see, this is a bad thing.

Not just in romantic relationships. You have, hopefully, told your kids that if anyone wants them to keep secrets from you, the parents, that is a bad person. If someone says after a fender bender, "No need to get the insurance company and the police involved," or a supervisor says, "No need for the union. Let's just keep this between us." A person who does that has a reason for trying to separate you from your alliances. He wants you weak. You should never get in a relationship where the other person wants you weak.

Unpredictable. In one of the worst types of violence cycles, the abuser is often nice for no reason. The violence is rarely random, since he or she needs a hook (see section 2.7). The being nice, with flattery and effusive gifts, is random. This is a powerful and subtle dynamic. People naturally find patterns. If you cannot find the pattern, you can't learn to work the pattern. If you can't work the pattern, you are helpless.

Everything is wrong. You'll see this with bad managers even more than in bad relationships. If you are chewed out or punished no matter what you do, your monkey, lizard, and human brain all learn that the best strategy is to do nothing. For the predator it makes a passive victim. For the manager it makes a passive workforce.

The combination of the last two, "everything is wrong" + "unpredictable" over the long term can groom a victim personality as described in appendix 1.

This is a two-way street. Recognizing a violent dynamic is not just about recognizing the violent one. There are also people who are violence magnets. People who are serially victimized or jump from abusive relationship to abusive relationship.

Two things. First, keep people like this out of your life. If your best friend somehow gets beat up at a bar every Saturday night, you don't go to bars with him. Violence in the past is the best indicator of violence in the future. If you are tempted to rescue a maiden in distress coming out of her fourth abusive relationship . . . just like the abuser, this is the tribal identity under which she knows how to function. Her monkey brain will eventually try to force you into the abuser role. Walk away.

Second, if you are one of these violence magnets, accept the fact. And change. It will be hard. Whether it is leaving a violent relationship or leaving the gang lifestyle, you must learn you can function in a better world, and then you must learn how. It will take an extraordinary act of will and probably cutting all ties to your previous world, but it can be done if you want it bad enough and are willing to pay the price.

Is This a Dangerous Place?

I've discussed this extensively in *Facing Violence*, so this will be a quick recap. Any place can be dangerous if you are specifically targeted, but it is rare for that to happen without your knowledge. Ever done anything that would get the mob to send an assassin after you? If not, you don't need a strategy for hit men. Ever pissed off anybody who learned to use a knife in prison? Then you don't have to worry about getting shanked.

There are only five types of places where violence is common.

1. Where young men gather in groups. Lots of testosterone, lots of stupidity. Lots of people strongly in their monkey brains attempting to establish status, get a reputation, and show off. In the worst case, they can push each other to greater and greater demonstrations of violence.

2. Where people get their minds altered. Drugs, alcohol, and even ritual drumming lower inhibition. There is no drug that makes you smarter. They make people stupid and they hamper judgment.

3. Where territories are in dispute. Gang turf wars. Battle zones. The territory doesn't have to be real—people, especially drunk young men, get in fights over sports a lot.

4. Where you don't know the rules. If you travel outside of tourist zones in foreign countries or go to areas in your hometown with a different population, you may be inadvertently rude. Probably not a big deal at the country club—they'll just snub you and whisper snide things. Possibly a big deal at a redneck watering hole. The first four are the places where social violence is likely to occur. The fifth:

5. Predatory violence happens in lonely places. Places with no witnesses.

It's unrealistic to suggest that you avoid all of these places. Just be on alert and take precautions when you decide to go. Again, there is far more information about this in *Facing Violence*.

Will This Situation Become Violent?

If the potential bad guy (the "threat," in law enforcement terms) is a predator, the situation is dangerous. The next section (appendix 2.4) will discuss distinguishing a predatory approach from a social approach.

Violence stemming from social levels, monkey-brain violence, generally requires certain factors:

1. The threat must be comfortable with violence as described in the first section of the appendix.

2. The threat must feel betrayed, feel humiliated, or have othered you.

Comfort level with violence has been discussed. If people feel humiliated or betrayed, they are likely to retaliate with the highest level of force they can muster. Humiliation and betrayal are two of the extraordinary circumstances that can jump a person up a level.

In other words, if you humiliate someone who is comfortable using a knife, there is a good possibility she will stab you. If you humiliate someone who is not, he may file a suit, or threaten to file a suit, or start a gossip campaign, or say things about you behind your back.

The second factor is the most important. It is also the one you can control, with the exception of othering, but othering can be noticed and monitored.

If you have an employee who works to make sure he is not a member of the tribe represented by your agency, that is something to watch. In order to keep his fellow employees at arm's length, the subject must insist on minimizing his connection with the group, usually by maximizing his connection to an outside group.

When people want to get along, they minimize differences and maximize similarities. When they want to other, they do the opposite.

If you invite someone out to lunch who has dietary restrictions— whether religious, personal ethics, or health based—if he or she minimizes those differences, merely looking for something acceptable on the menu and only mentioning it if asked, that person is cementing ties with you. On the other hand, the person who makes the meal about the dietary restrictions is sending you the signal that his identity is based on another tribe. He will actively work to prevent bonding with your group.

So if you want to know if the person you fired will come back and shoot you, the first question is, "Is he comfortable enough with violence to shoot?" Remember you don't know his background. Most of the shooters I know are either quiet or friendly people who try to get along. That sweet Southern belle may have been shooting big game since she was a child.

The second question: "Has he actively worked to other you and his fellow employees?"

The third and most important question: "Was the firing humiliating or could it be seen as a betrayal?"

There is a vast difference between laying off the lowest-seniority member after months of warning memos and laying off a loyal worker two days after you promised his job was safe. There is a difference between bringing someone into the office to give him the sack and firing him, with an insult, in front of his friends.

The monkey brain doesn't deal with humiliation well at all. It can see it as an attempt to kill, and it can incite extreme defensiveness or retaliation.

Outside the workforce, the same general rules apply. This means in most cases, if the situation gets violent, you have contributed to that.

> *In southern Europe, when I was teaching a self-defense course, one of the students caught me at the break and asked for some personal instructions. He wanted specific self-defense techniques in case his mistress's husband should catch them—since, as he said it, any man in that situation would be mad enough to kill.*

You don't want to be stabbed? Don't be the kind of person who makes people that angry. You understand the monkey mind. Respect tribal boundaries. Never make it personal. Never betray, since a sense of betrayal will draw the highest sanction in any culture. Never humiliate.

I'm assuming you are an intelligent adult and I don't have to say the super-obvious things, like, "If someone points a gun at you, you are in danger." That said, if someone points a gun at you and you say something humiliating, like, "You haven't got the guts to shoot me," you are in much more danger.

> I tell rookie officers to never humiliate and never cause unnecessary pain. It will not make the criminal a better person. If you are trying to teach a lesson, he won't learn it. He will confirm his worldview that everyone is just as bad or worse than he is. And, more important, if you take his manhood, he will get it back. Not on you, on someone weaker. Every act of humiliation guarantees someone down the line, probably his wife or child, will be beaten to assuage his ego.

I'm going to end this subsection with Peyton Quinn's rules of violence. Peyton is one of the pioneers of the reality-based self-defense movement. This is for social violence, monkey-stuff:

1. Do not deny it is happening.

2. Don't insult him.

3. Don't challenge him (or accept his challenge).

4. Always give a face-saving way out.

Am I Being Targeted For Violence?

Most violence is social, intended to promote the good of the group, and to minimize violence. As such, there are far more angry words and gestures than there is actual harm done between people. Those words and gestures are threat displays and are intended to prevent violence by threatening violence.

Asocial violence follows a different pattern. It is about hunting, not about communication, and the predator works to send deceptive signals or no signal at all.

In either case, watch for signs of adrenaline.

Most people can't fight "cold." They need the emotional edge of fear or anger to get over the taboos involved in hurting people. Not everyone, but almost everyone. Even very experienced fighters, whether good guys or bad guys, want to be "in the zone," just like any other athlete. Part of being in the zone is an optimum level of adrenalization.

I'll use adrenaline throughout this as easy shorthand, but know that the survival stress response is caused by a slew of hormones and neurotransmitters, not just adrenaline.

There are lots of symptoms of adrenaline—breathing changes, pulse rate, pupils—that I don't care about because you can't see them. Signs are distinguished from symptoms in that signs are what an outside observer can see.

There are several common adrenaline signs:

Gross motor activity. Under an adrenaline dump, you want to move. Pace. Flex.

Clumsiness. The big muscles want to move, but circulation is cut off to the periphery, and so people get clumsy, shake, and drop things.

Voice gets higher pitched.

Swallowing and licking lips. Or drinking a lot of water if available. Adrenaline burns up a lot of water and makes you very thirsty. Sidenote: Tardive dyskinesia is one of the side effects of long-term use of psych meds. Street people call it the "Thorazine twitch." Tardive dyskinesia also involves a lot of lip licking with darting tongue movements but will also have sharp twitches and (usually) hard blinking.

Rhythmic movement. Almost every person I've seen under an adrenaline dump does something rhythmic. Many tap their fingers (especially if they are trying to hide fear or anger). Or they bounce on their toes. Some hum. Not usually whistling, because the mouth is too dry to whistle.

Color change. Getting red is part of the threat display. These guys don't tend to bother me. They might get stupid and become dangerous, but that's not the sign I'm looking for. When a threat goes pale, things are about to step off. The paleness, of course, comes from peripheral vasoconstriction. The body is trying to make sure that if the saber-toothed tiger gets an arm or a leg, you won't bleed too much. Think of sudden pallor as the body's clearing the deck for action. Action is imminent.

Danger happens at the intersection of adrenaline and purpose. A drowning man will be adrenalized and have the purpose of breathing, which makes you look like a flotation device. A mugger needs money for drugs and will get his adrenaline into the zone to do the crime.

Someone engaged in social violence generally won't try to hide his adrenaline. It's part of the show. The two groups that will try to hide it are criminals and professionals.

Professionals (like bouncers lighting cigarettes to prove their hands aren't shaking) tend to have elaborately relaxed body language. Their job is to defuse the situation if at all possible, so they will close the distance and get in position while giving relaxed and nonthreatening body language. They will be focused on the threat, however. If you see someone who should be showing the signs and isn't and he is focused, assume you have a professional. (As opposed to someone who should be adrenalized and is oblivious, in which case you have your basic nitwit.)

Criminals have to close the distance and set you at your ease. They have to appear *not* to be focused on you, and they want to control the adrenaline. Many will engage in self-calming behavior. When your kids are hurt or afraid, you pick them up and hug them, right?

You basically pet them like small animals. Self-calming is doing that solo. Rubbing the face or neck is the most common.

There is one more professional reaction, but not necessarily criminal. One of the things with criminals is that they can time when to attack, so they can control their own adrenaline. They can get themselves excited (with visualization, ritual, or self-talk) to raise their adrenaline, and they can get the adrenaline under control by waiting a little longer, breathing, or other self-calming behaviors.

Victims don't get that choice. When the threat arises, they get an adrenaline dump. If *you* are a force professional (LEO, soldier, bouncer), your job will be to accost people. From their point of view, you are the threat. You will use the same techniques bad guys use to control your own adrenaline (and hopefully, you will use these techniques more consciously, because you were trained and taught more effectively). But the people you confront will not have that option. They will get an adrenaline dump.

If they go pale, things are on the edge of going bad.

If, however, the subject goes pale *and relaxes and his eyes are unfocussed*, you may be in for a very bad day. Most people tense and shrink up when the adrenaline hits hard. If you see relaxation and the thousand-yard stare, you have stumbled on someone with extensive experience with adrenaline. He knows how to use every last drop of it. If you see this, you may well be in for the fight of your life. On the good side, if you see this, the subject is still thinking clearly enough that you can reason. You can rarely do that with the ones who go white and tense up.

Distinguishing Social and Asocial

Are you being targeted by a predator? The keys are the presence of witnesses, the body language, the distance, and the foot position.

If monkey-level violence is in the air, there will generally be an audience. The threat will be standing in front of you and will tend to start out of arm's reach. His feet will be square to you. He will tend to be up on his toes. It makes him look bigger.

A predator will rarely approach this way, primarily because it is stupid and inefficient to victimize people from the front, with plenty of warning and a bad foot position for fighting.

The predator doesn't want an audience. Audiences magically turn into witnesses for violent crime. He must get close to you. If someone closes in a lonely place, it is a bad sign.

Each culture has an acceptable distance for strangers. Facing a stranger, in northern Europe and the US, the distance is just beyond arm's reach. If a stranger is asking for directions, this is the distance he will choose.

This imaginary five-foot bubble is not round, however. Strangers can get quite close on the flanks without making you uncomfortable. Experiment with this in crowded elevators. So criminals will tend to sidle up to you rather than face you square-on. It gets them in striking range without setting off your alarms.

The third sign is foot placement. You are more powerful and move faster if an imaginary line drawn from foot to foot would point at your target. This is what we call a bladed stance. Cops and criminals stand that way routinely, but it is very rare in social interactions.

Last detail: Frequently, just before the assault, the bad guy will give one look around, a witness check to see if anyone has appeared who might interfere.

APPENDIX 3   THE LOVE SCRIPT

There is a method to make people fall in love with you. It is simple and it is under your conscious control. It is not ethical and I do not want you practicing it to hurt others.

This is "falling in love," not love. There are many different emotions and relationships that fall under the word "love."

What does falling in love feel like? What are the physical signs and symptoms? The most gorgeous person in the world shoots you a sly smile. What do you feel?

Your palms sweat. Your mouth goes dry. Your heart speeds up. Maybe a queasy stomach and weak knees. What is that? Adrenaline.

You would get those same symptoms if you saw a bear.

The James-Lange theory of emotion is that an event happens (shy smile or a bear), your body dumps a mix of hormones and neurotransmitters (which we'll just call adrenaline for shorthand), and you then name your feelings. Love or fear are labels we supply to a chemical event. The chemical event is a data point and a fact. The label makes it an emotion.

In order to make someone fall in love with you, there must be some slight interest or attraction. That is the only part of the process that you can't control. If the interest is there, if you give enough clues to believe there is a chance at a relationship but never enough for the other person to get confident, he or she will begin to feel a constant trickle of adrenaline in your presence. That person will call this falling for you.

I'm going to corroborate this from two directions in a minute, but first, go over your own personal history. The people you have fallen for and the people who have fallen for you. See if it reads true.

And if you've ever wondered why smart people so often fall for jerks and self-centered bimbos . . .

Corroboration: Anytime you have heard someone say, "I still love you, but I'm not in love with you anymore," or "I [we] fell out of love," or "The magic is gone," it happened when the relationship got stable enough that the adrenaline cut off.

The second corroboration is rare, but Hollywood likes this trope. Two people, best friends, completely compatible . . . but there has never been "that spark," and so they stay friends for years. They have a stable friendship until one of them meets someone else, maybe gets engaged. The fear of loss triggers an adrenaline cascade and they realize it was "true love" all along.

This is the power of scripts, and there are a lot of implications here. Some minor, some very important.

The minor one: Often the difference between good and bad fiction is whether the characters stayed within natural scripts. Characters who don't follow the scripts feel wrong and the story feels off. Without the life-threatening dynamic between their families, Romeo and Juliet would be two rich kids hooking up. Initial love, in fiction or real life, always has this element of fear.

Far more important: Our most profound, most emotional and spiritual events are driven by mechanical, monkey-brain programs. A script starts with a look, and you get adrenaline. She says, "I like you but . . ." and the "but" drives another adrenaline spike. And this becomes an epic love story, either the grandest adventure or the biggest mistake of your life.

And it was all predictable. Manipulable.

That gives you a choice. A human-brain choice. To decide if it is special, or if it is not. I chose special.

Second incredible implication, harking back to section 2.6.2: Don't Take It Personally. You don't hate anyone. A script has been running and with that script comes a certain amount of adrenaline, and your monkey brain labeled it hate, and that is all the validity your monkey brain needs.

If love can be this mechanical, if love can be a choice, so can hate. You don't need to hate anyone. Change the script and you will change the emotion.

AFTERWORD

Your world has changed. Not so much, really. Maybe some of the details in the section on violence were new, but almost everything in this book is stuff you live every day. You already knew this.

But now you see it. In seeing it, you can make connections. You can predict scripts and you can change them. You can choose whether to play the monkey game.

Most of the time the monkey game is good. We wouldn't be able to live in society without our little rituals of friendship and acknowledgment. A society where everyone is in the human brain all the time would feel sterile, empty, and maybe pointless.

But sometimes the monkey gets in the way. You can see that now. And if you see it, you can make a choice.

Your world has changed; and in a lot of ways, it will be more annoying. Political debates that may have once fascinated you will seem to be about 5 percent information and 95 percent tribalism. You will watch people destroy themselves on petty monkey problems that they could easily sidestep. Watch people agonize and take things personally that were never personal.

This will become your next monkey trap: you will see all of this and begin to believe you are a superior monkey because you can see and others cannot.

That's your monkey brain. It's not going away. But you have a few more tools to make it happy and get the job done.

GLOSSARY

active listening. Stopping one's internal monologue and actually paying attention in a conversation.

affordances. The possibilities seen in a situation.

antisocial personality disorder. A personality type that disregards rules, social norms, and (on a scale) lacks empathy for others.

asocial. Not antisocial. Asocial is not recognizing, either through inability or choice, the humanity of the person one is interacting with.

asocial violence. Violence with an asocial mind-set, not recognizing the humanity of your victim. Asocial violence is not great rage, but simple efficiency. Just a job.

belongingness. In Maslow's theory, the deep need to belong to a group. No idea why he couldn't just say "belonging."

domestic violence. Abuse between family or household members.

coercion. Making someone do something he or she would rather not do.

Conflict Communications (ConCom). This program. Understanding and manipulating the source of the real disagreement.

de-escalation. Jargon term for preventing a hostile situation from escalating to violence.

ego. In Freud's lexicon, the rational part of the mind. In common terms, pride and self-centeredness. In practical ConCom terms, your monkey brain.

emotionally disturbed person (EDP). In real life you often can't tell if you're dealing with someone very angry or afraid, someone with a mental illness, or someone having a bad drug reaction. EDP is the current catch-all phrase.

excited delirium. A medical condition in which body temperature is extremely elevated and the subject is often incredibly violent.

fight/flight/freeze responses. Natural animal responses to sudden danger. Freeze comes first, then flight, and only then fight.

forced teaming. Using verbal tricks to induce the assumption of common cause in the other person's mind. "We're in this together."

goal-oriented groups. Groups centered on achieving objectives. Something external to the group (e.g., a work product or fighting crime) is the highest priority and reason for the group.

hooks. Something to hang the blame on. People who do bad things seek justification. A person who wishes to harm you will often try to get you to do or say something he or she can use to blame you. Note: The intent to do harm comes before the search for a justification. The justification is never the reason.

human brain. In ConCom terms, the part of your mind that solves problems with reason and insight.

id. In Freudian terms, your dark, animalistic desires.

inner critic. The voice in the heads of writers and artists that always whispers, "This isn't good enough. *You* aren't good enough."

labeling. Categorizing someone as a thing (e.g., asshole) or as a member of a group (e.g., liberal/conservative). A mechanism that prevents the human brain from listening.

leadership. Getting things done through force of personality.

lizard brain. In ConCom terms, the deepest part of your brain. Your survival instincts. The part of you that is a ruthless animal.

loansharking. Doing nice things, apparently for no reason, which sets a feeling of obligation in the other person's mind.

longevity-oriented groups. Groups centered on maintaining the group into the future with minimal change.

management. Getting things done by creating a procedure to be followed.

monkey brain. The social and emotional parts of the mind.

monkey dance. Ritualized fighting between young men.

mores. The elements of proper behavior in a given society. The unwritten rule about how things are done. Pronounced like the moray eel.

Maslow's hierarchy of needs. A theory of motivation postulating that survival needs precede security needs, security needs precede belongingness needs, and esteem needs precede the ability to achieve one's potential.

othering. Convincing oneself that someone else is less or other than a human.

scripts. In ConCom, predictable patterns of interaction.

shadow community. The collection of voices in your head that critique, modify, and sometimes seem to control your behavior.

snowflakes. In ConCom, people with very low official status but very high value to a group are often stressed by the disparity.

social. Interactions in which the other person is treated as a full fellow human.

social violence. A form of communication. Violence in which sending a message is the primary goal.

status checking. When the monkey brain is confronted with unusual behavior from a known person, it is compelled to stop and try to see if change is coming.

superego. Freud's term for your internalized rules of good—your conscience.

tactical apology. Apologizing for effect instead of for your actions.

threat assessment. Judging the level and type of danger you may be facing.

toxic personalities. People who actively sabotage the groups they work and live with.

unsolicited promises. A tactic wherein someone promises not to do a certain behavior without being asked for such a promise. Usually a tactic to elicit information or a concession in return.

untouchables. People who work hard at being unpleasant to work with, supervise, or just be around. Many are toxic personalities.

violence. There are lots of dictionary definitions. For our purposes, violence is a level on both the continuum of conflict and the continuum of coercion. But each of us will have different criteria for what rises to the level of violence.

ya. Short for "you." The norm with friendly interaction.

ABOUT THE COURSE

This manual is based on the Conflict Communications course I created with Marc MacYoung. In 2009, Marc called me up—he had recently read my first book, *Meditations on Violence*, and had been in Europe teaching police officers.

"Hey, I was teaching a de-escalation course and realized a lot of the material was coming out of your book *Meditations on Violence*. Would you be interested in collaborating on a course for cops on talking bad guys down?" Marc asked.

Hmmm. Marc MacYoung. One of the pioneers of reality-based self-defense. The first person, as far as I know, to actually point out that self-defense and martial arts aren't the same thing. Hell yeah.

And I had just finished the draft of *Facing Violence*, which broke social and asocial conflicts down as qualitative differences. That would be the starting point.

The test runs of the class were phenomenal. The most common feedback was excited. As one of the first said, "Yeah, it'll work on criminals. But guys, this explains my boss. This explains my wife." We'd stumbled on something much bigger than we imagined.

Marc MacYoung: http://nnsd.com

Rory Miller: http://chirontraining.com/Site/ConCom.html
https://www.facebook.com/pages/Conflict-Communications/338132414527

BIBLIOGRAPHY

Chun Siong Soon, Marcel Brass, Hans-Jochen Heinze, and John-Dylan Haynes. "Unconscious Determinants of Free Decisions in the Human Brain," *Nature Neuroscience* 11: 543–545 (2008).

DeBecker, Gavin. *The Gift of Fear and Other Survival Signals That Can Save Your Life.* NY: Dell Publishing, 1997.

Gladwell, Malcolm. *Blink: The Power of Thinking Without Thinking.* NY: Little, Brown and Company, 2005.

Hatzfled, Jean. *Machete Season: The Killers in Rwanda Speak.* English translation NY: Farrar, Straus and Giroux, 2005.

Henrich, Joseph, Steven J. Heine, and Ara Norenzayan. "The Weirdest People in the World?" *RatSWD Working Paper No. 139,* May 7, 2010.

Howe, MSG Paul R. *Leadership and Training for the Fight: A Few Thoughts on Leadership and Training from a Former Special Operations Soldier.* Bloomington: AuthorHouse, 2006.

Kennedy, Burt (director). *Support Your Local Sheriff.* Hollywood: MGM, 1968.

Maslow, Abraham H. "A Theory of Human Motivation," *Psychological Review*, 50: 370–396 (1943).

Miller, Rory (ed.). *Campfire Tales from Hell.* Los Gatos, CA: SmashWords ebook courtesy of Marc MacYoung, 2012.

Miller, Rory. *Facing Violence.* Wolfeboro, NH: YMAA, 2011.

Miller, Rory. *Meditations on Violence.* Wolfeboro, NH: YMAA, 2008.

Miller, Rory. *Talking Them Through: Crisis Communication with the Emotionally Disturbed and Mentally Ill.* Ebook available through most suppliers, 2012.

Twigger, Robert. *Angry White Pyjamas: A Scrawny Oxford Poet Takes Lessons from the Tokyo Riot Police.* NY: HarperCollins, 1997.

Westen, Drew. *The Political Brain: The Role of Emotion in Deciding the Fate of the Nation.* Philadelphia: Public Affairs, 2007.

INDEX

ABOUT THE AUTHOR

Rory Miller is the award-winning author of *Meditations on Violence, Facing Violence, Force Decisions*, and *Violence: A Writer's Guide*. He is the coauthor, with Lawrence Kane, of *Scaling Force*.

A former corrections sergeant, tactical team leader, and contractor in Iraq, he now lives quietly on his acreage in the Pacific Northwest, writing and teaching seminars internationally.

He can be contacted through his website at
http://chirontraining.com
He does his thinking out loud at
http://chirontraining.blogspot.com

BOOKS FROM YMAA

6 HEALING MOVEMENTS
101 REFLECTIONS ON TAI CHI CHUAN
108 INSIGHTS INTO TAI CHI CHUAN
ADVANCING IN TAE KWON DO
ANALYSIS OF SHAOLIN CHIN NA 2ND ED
ANCIENT CHINESE WEAPONS
ART OF HOJO UNDO
ARTHRITIS RELIEF, 3RD ED.
BACK PAIN RELIEF, 2ND ED.
BAGUAZHANG, 2ND ED.
CARDIO KICKBOXING ELITE
CHIN NA IN GROUND FIGHTING
CHINESE FAST WRESTLING
CHINESE FITNESS
CHINESE TUI NA MASSAGE
CHOJUN
COMPREHENSIVE APPLICATIONS OF SHAOLIN
   CHIN NA
CONFLICT COMMUNICATION
CROCODILE AND THE CRANE: A NOVEL
CUTTING SEASON: A XENON PEARL MARTIAL
   ARTS THRILLER
DESHI: A CONNOR BURKE MARTIAL ARTS THRILLER
DIRTY GROUND
DR. WU'S HEAD MASSAGE
DUKKHA REVERB
DUKKHA, THE SUFFERING: AN EYE FOR AN EYE
DUKKHA UNLOADED
ENZAN: THE FAR MOUNTAIN, A CONNOR BURKE MARTIAL
   ARTS THRILLER
ESSENCE OF SHAOLIN WHITE CRANE
EXPLORING TAI CHI
FACING VIOLENCE
FIGHT LIKE A PHYSICIST
FIGHTING ARTS
FIRST DEFENSE
FORCE DECISIONS: A CITIZENS GUIDE
FOX BORROWS THE TIGER'S AWE
INSIDE TAI CHI
KAGE: THE SHADOW, A CONNOR BURKE MARTIAL ARTS
   THRILLER
KATA AND THE TRANSMISSION OF KNOWLEDGE
KRAV MAGA: WEAPON DEFENSES
LITTLE BLACK BOOK OF VIOLENCE
LIUHEBAFA FIVE CHARACTER SECRETS
MARTIAL ARTS ATHLETE
MARTIAL ARTS INSTRUCTION
MARTIAL WAY AND ITS VIRTUES
MASK OF THE KING
MEDITATIONS ON VIOLENCE
MIND/BODY FITNESS
THE MIND INSIDE TAI CHI
MUGAI RYU
NATURAL HEALING WITH QIGONG
NORTHERN SHAOLIN SWORD, 2ND ED.
OKINAWA'S COMPLETE KARATE SYSTEM: ISSHIN RYU
POWER BODY
PRINCIPLES OF TRADITIONAL CHINESE MEDICINE

QIGONG FOR HEALTH & MARTIAL ARTS 2ND ED.
QIGONG FOR LIVING
QIGONG FOR TREATING COMMON AILMENTS
QIGONG MASSAGE
QIGONG MEDITATION: EMBRYONIC BREATHING
QIGONG MEDITATION: SMALL CIRCULATION
QIGONG, THE SECRET OF YOUTH: DA MO'S CLASSICS
QUIET TEACHER: A XENON PEARL MARTIAL ARTS
   THRILLER
RAVEN'S WARRIOR
ROOT OF CHINESE QIGONG, 2ND ED.
SCALING FORCE
SENSEI: A CONNOR BURKE MARTIAL ARTS THRILLER
SHIHAN TE: THE BUNKAI OF KATA
SHIN GI TAI: KARATE TRAINING FOR BODY, MIND, AND
   SPIRIT
SIMPLE CHINESE MEDICINE
SIMPLE QIGONG EXERCISES FOR HEALTH, 3RD ED.
SIMPLIFIED TAI CHI CHUAN, 3RD ED.
SUDDEN DAWN: THE EPIC JOURNEY OF BODHIDHARMA
SUNRISE TAI CHI
SUNSET TAI CHI
SURVIVING ARMED ASSAULTS
TAE KWON DO: THE KOREAN MARTIAL ART
TAEKWONDO BLACK BELT POOMSAE
TAEKWONDO: A PATH TO EXCELLENCE
TAEKWONDO: ANCIENT WISDOM FOR THE MODERN
   WARRIOR
TAEKWONDO: DEFENSES AGAINST WEAPONS
TAEKWONDO: SPIRIT AND PRACTICE
TAO OF BIOENERGETICS
TAI CHI BALL QIGONG: FOR HEALTH AND MARTIAL ARTS
TAI CHI BOOK
TAI CHI CHIN NA: THE SEIZING ART OF TAI CHI CHUAN
TAI CHI CHUAN CLASSICAL YANG STYLE (REVISED
   EDITION)
TAI CHI CHUAN MARTIAL APPLICATIONS
TAI CHI CHUAN MARTIAL POWER
TAI CHI CONNECTIONS
TAI CHI DYNAMICS
TAI CHI QIGONG, 3RD ED.
TAI CHI SECRETS OF THE ANCIENT MASTERS
TAI CHI SECRETS OF THE WU & LI STYLES
TAI CHI SECRETS OF THE WU STYLE
TAI CHI SECRETS OF THE YANG STYLE
TAI CHI SWORD: CLASSICAL YANG STYLE
TAI CHI WALKING
TAIJIQUAN THEORY OF DR. YANG, JWING-MING
TENGU: THE MOUNTAIN GOBLIN, A CONNOR BURKE
   MARTIAL ARTS THRILLER
TRADITIONAL CHINESE HEALTH SECRETS
TRADITIONAL TAEKWONDO
WAY OF KATA
WAY OF KENDO AND KENJITSU
WAY OF SANCHIN KATA
WAY TO BLACK BELT
WESTERN HERBS FOR MARTIAL ARTISTS
WILD GOOSE QIGONG

continued on next page . . .

DVDS FROM YMAA

ADVANCED PRACTICAL CHIN NA IN-DEPTH

ANALYSIS OF SHAOLIN CHIN NA

BAGUAZHANG: EMEI BAGUAZHANG

CHEN STYLE TAIJIQUAN

CHIN NA IN-DEPTH COURSES 1—4

CHIN NA IN-DEPTH COURSES 5—8

CHIN NA IN-DEPTH COURSES 9—12

FACING VIOLENCE: 7 THINGS A MARTIAL ARTIST MUST KNOW

FIVE ANIMAL SPORTS

JOINT LOCKS

KNIFE DEFENSE: TRADITIONAL TECHNIQUES AGAINST A DAGGER

KUNG FU BODY CONDITIONING 1

KUNG FU BODY CONDITIONING 2

KUNG FU FOR KIDS

KUNG FU FOR TEENS

INFIGHTING

LOGIC OF VIOLENCE

MERIDIAN QIGONG

NEIGONG FOR MARTIAL ARTS

NORTHERN SHAOLIN SWORD : SAN CAI JIAN, KUN WU JIAN, QI MEN JIAN

QIGONG MASSAGE

QIGONG FOR HEALING

QIGONG FOR LONGEVITY

QIGONG FOR WOMEN

SABER FUNDAMENTAL TRAINING

SANCHIN KATA: TRADITIONAL TRAINING FOR KARATE POWER

SHAOLIN KUNG FU FUNDAMENTAL TRAINING: COURSES 1 & 2

SHAOLIN LONG FIST KUNG FU: BASIC SEQUENCES

SHAOLIN LONG FIST KUNG FU: INTERMEDIATE SEQUENCES

SHAOLIN LONG FIST KUNG FU: ADVANCED SEQUENCES 1

SHAOLIN LONG FIST KUNG FU: ADVANCED SEQUENCES 2

SHAOLIN SABER: BASIC SEQUENCES

SHAOLIN STAFF: BASIC SEQUENCES

SHAOLIN WHITE CRANE GONG FU BASIC TRAINING: COURSES 1 & 2

SHAOLIN WHITE CRANE GONG FU BASIC TRAINING: COURSES 3 & 4

SHUAI JIAO: KUNG FU WRESTLING

SIMPLE QIGONG EXERCISES FOR ARTHRITIS RELIEF

SIMPLE QIGONG EXERCISES FOR BACK PAIN RELIEF

SIMPLIFIED TAI CHI CHUAN: 24 & 48 POSTURES

SUNRISE TAI CHI

SUNSET TAI CHI

SWORD: FUNDAMENTAL TRAINING

TAEKWONDO KORYO POOMSAE

TAI CHI BALL QIGONG: COURSES 1 & 2

TAI CHI BALL QIGONG: COURSES 3 & 4

TAI CHI CHUAN CLASSICAL YANG STYLE

TAI CHI CONNECTIONS

TAI CHI ENERGY PATTERNS

TAI CHI FIGHTING SET

TAI CHI PUSHING HANDS: COURSES 1 & 2

TAI CHI PUSHING HANDS: COURSES 3 & 4

TAI CHI SWORD: CLASSICAL YANG STYLE

TAI CHI SYMBOL: YIN YANG STICKING HANDS

TAIJI & SHAOLIN STAFF: FUNDAMENTAL TRAINING

TAIJI CHIN NA IN-DEPTH

TAIJI 37 POSTURES MARTIAL APPLICATIONS

TAIJI SABER CLASSICAL YANG STYLE

TAIJI WRESTLING

UNDERSTANDING QIGONG 1: WHAT IS QI? • HUMAN QI CIRCULATORY SYSTEM

UNDERSTANDING QIGONG 2: KEY POINTS • QIGONG BREATHING

UNDERSTANDING QIGONG 3: EMBRYONIC BREATHING

UNDERSTANDING QIGONG 4: FOUR SEASONS QIGONG

UNDERSTANDING QIGONG 5: SMALL CIRCULATION

UNDERSTANDING QIGONG 6: MARTIAL QIGONG BREATHING

WHITE CRANE HARD & SOFT QIGONG

WUDANG KUNG FU: FUNDAMENTAL TRAINING

WUDANG SWORD

WUDANG TAIJIQUAN

XINGYIQUAN

YANG TAI CHI FOR BEGINNERS

more products available from . . .
YMAA Publication Center, Inc. 楊氏東方文化出版中心

1-800-669-8892 • info@ymaa.com • www.ymaa.com